"This is My Body...
Creativity,
Clay, and Change

MARJORY ZOET BANKSON

with Foreword by M.C. Richards, author of CENTERING

SAN DIEGO, CALIFORNIA

LURAMEDIA™

Other Books by Marjory Zoet Bankson:
SEASONS OF FRIENDSHIP: Naomi and Ruth as a Pattern
BRAIDED STREAMS: Esther and a Woman's Way of Growing

Copyright © 1993 LuraMedia
San Diego, California
International Copyright Secured
Publisher's Catalog Number LM-638
Printed and bound in the United States of America

Cover art by Sara Steele, "Solar Plexus/Iron Ball,"
from the Women Against Abuse series.
Copyright © 1992 by Sara Steele. All Rights Reserved.

Cover design by Tom Jackson, Philadelphia.

Chapter illustrations by Marjory Zoet Bankson.
Monoprints created with ink on glass;
prints made on rice paper.

LuraMedia
7060 Miramar Road, Suite 104
San Diego, CA 92121

Library of Congress Cataloging-in-Publication-Data
Bankson, Marjory Zoet.
    This is my body : creativity, clay, and change / by Marjory
Zoet Bankson.
        p.   cm.
    ISBN 0-931055-94-6
    1. Spiritual life--Christianity. 2. Bankson, Marjory Zoet.
3. Women in the Bible--Meditations. 4. Art pottery.
5. Creative ability--Religious aspects--Christianity--
Meditations.   I. Title.
BV4501.2.B3825   1993   92-35244
248.4--dc20   CIP

for Jean and Louie Mideke,
with thanks

CONTENTS

FOREWORD

CLAY AND POTTERY have a way of leading us to parables and metaphors, whether we are potters or poets or preachers or teachers or lovers or just folks. Though the basic image of this book is our clay body and its transformations, *"This Is My Body. . . "* moves through that image into fields of human concern. People who work with clay for the first time are often struck by the sense of intimacy and creative hope that quickens in their souls, however shyly. People who have never touched clay, and probably never will, are often enriched by a sense of depth and meaning, hard to speak about, but lingering around the neck of a Chinese vase or the energetic handle of a pottery mug. There is a strange and unmistakable aura about this craft and this substance. After all, we are made of it. And likewise, whether or not we think of ourselves as religious or Christian, there is something about "life" that feeds us in bread and wine and fellowship, as it did Christ's disciples. Marjory Zoet Bankson has been deeply inspired by the experiences of being a potter, and has let that inspiration rise and fill a picture of the human being, created and recreated in the divine fire. If readers can follow with "soft eyes" the journey of craftswoman and minister, they will receive surprising and original and imaginative gifts.

This book could only have been written out of deeply committed, personal experience: thirty years as a potter (an artist in clay) and a lifetime journey from biblical roots into contemporary religious authenticity. Marjory Bankson has found her way into a personal ministry that includes in its wholeness her vocation as a potter. She recognizes that the immediacy of clay forms a spontaneous and intimate connection with our bodies. Out of this integration, she forms an image of our human journey into sexuality, soul, and spirit.

"As my inner hand begins to define the space inside, I am aware of a 'spirit force' inside of me, longing for shape and form in the world. As my outer or centering hand supports the thinning clay wall, I am aware of the need for structure, commitment, and routine. . . . Inner and outer pressures combine to shape my soul, stretching me beyond the predictable balance of a straightsided cylinder toward my unique shape and purpose." (93-94)

Drawn to the lives of biblical women who helped her reclaim her feminine sense of self, Bankson creates fourteen dramatic monologues of Hebrew Testament and New Testament women, showing in each pair an analogy with the process of making a pot: preparing the ground, kneading, centering, shaping, finishing, glazing, firing — experiencing inner change as the vessel is transformed through the stages of its becoming. Through *touch*, we become connected to *heart*.

"Clay was my teacher, and from the clay process I have drawn a model for change. . . . I am speaking of internal change that results in a new form and shape in the physical world. That is the heart of this book: conscious, embodied change." (15)

When we commit pots to the fire of the kiln, "the prize for this commitment is transformation — a new internal structure"! (166) What an extraordinary focus on the actual changing of substance, and what a disciplined insistence on inner changes of habits and assumptions that underlie our behavior. "No matter how often I fire, opening the kiln is like rolling away the stone and experiencing resurrection first hand!" (169)

The clay body is earth's gift to us. Bread and wine are Christ's body given to us, which we may remember in a communion with others. "This is my body," he said as he broke bread and gave it to his disciples. "Do this in remembrance of me."

Many potters may be unused to recognizing in the body of their clay such sacred resonances. They can be enriched by the significance Bankson names in each gesture and aspect of the craft. The seven stages of clay are seven archetypal stages of becoming human. Sensitivity and imagination combine with self-valuing to create a wholeness. Bankson's potter's wheel has become a pulpit. She literally takes her wheel into the sacred space and speaks from it.

Marjory Zoet Bankson preaches and teaches — brings us to the communion table to be body to one another in new ways. I am very moved by the story of her life she tells here. She has taught me through friendship, as well, to be awestruck at how God loves to create through her. That "spirit force" inside of her indeed looks for shape and form in the world — and finds it. How inspired and inventive and faithful is her "Faith at Work." This book is a ministry, bringing readers to awareness in their own bodies and to compassionate sharing with others.

M.C. Richards, Ph.D.
Author of CENTERING
Kimberton Hills, Pennsylvania

PROLOGUE

IT IS CHRISTMAS, and once again the baby Jesus is plaguing my mind with impossibility. Could it be true that God was once this child? If Herod had succeeded in killing him with all the other innocents who were slain, would God be dead? What is the meaning of Jesus as a crying, cooing infant?

Each year the manger scene confronts my faith at a basic level. Was Jesus really one with God from the very beginning? Or do we only count his life as fully divine after his baptism? Or after the resurrection? Was the baby simply full of potential for being the Messiah? What about his body as an adolescent or young adult? What about his sexuality? And more importantly (to me), what does the physical body of Jesus have to do with my own body as an expression of God's intent for human life?

It was clay, not communion, that called my attention to the sacramental words, "This is my body . . . " because clay challenged my body. When I started working with clay in 1965, it demanded much of my body: balance, grace, agility, and a strong back for lifting the fifty-pound boxes that the clay came in. As a graduate student and then a high school teacher, I was used to working with my head, not with my whole body. In fact, I was quite unconscious of my body. I had strong feelings that seemed to come from my body, and I was glad for good health, which I took for granted, but my sense of being and reality was not grounded in my flesh and bones. My spiritual life felt quite separate from what was happening in my physical body.

Although my head was critical to my sense of identity, I did not know how to listen for my body's speech, nor did I value bodily signs except to blame myself for "overdoing" when I got an occasional cold. No wonder I did not pay any attention to the embodiment of Christ or the difference between men and women in the Church. All the focus of my spiritual life was on transcendence and a symbolic under-standing of the Last Supper as word and sign . . . until the clay awakened my fingertips and arms and shoulders and hips and legs and feet. Then, suddenly, I was curious about the part that my body had in God's realm.

My body. A woman's body. Loved by my husband and my parents, but rejected by the Church for ordination — or even for passing the collection plate as I was growing up. Good, in the eyes of my authority figures, for married sex and bearing children, but not good for independent travel or contact sports. I began to suspect that I was caring for others to avoid being in touch with my own body. I could identify with the brokenness of Jesus' body because my own felt scattered and unrecognizable in little pieces, consumed by others in a million different ways. I did not know much about my body as an expression of wholeness, though, and I wanted to change that.

Clay helped me to discover my body and my creativity because clay is direct, sensual, and dimensional — as we are. Clay also invited me into awareness of my soul, where spirit and body join in the substantial world. M.C. Richards, author of *Centering*, first introduced me to the concept of soul making in 1978 at Pendle Hill, a Quaker retreat center near Philadelphia. Using Jung's ideas of Soul and Self, she invited us to reflect on our pinched pots as an expression of creativity and imagination. Her work and words have continued to inspire my reflections, and I am grateful for the indelible mark she has made on my soul's journey. Since then, I have been encouraged to explore this theme of soul making in the writings of James Hillman, Alan Jones, and Thomas Moore's recent book, *Care of the Soul,* where he identifies soul work as the "vernacular speech" of the spirit. Soul making is earthy and substantial, creative and sorrowful, involved with birthing and dying.

CREATIVITY

As I learned to center the clay, pull a cylinder, trim and finish each pot, and finally to fire them in a kiln, I also learned the deep joy of my creativity. I loved the rhythm and routine of working alone and then interacting with people while selling my pots. I began to enjoy the stimulation of chance and change in the pottery studio and the marketplace.

I learned to trust the source of my creativity and not grieve the failures too much, because more would come. I also began to recognize that death and destruction were part of the creative process and to see that my body was part of the larger rhythm of endings and beginnings. Clay took me downward and inward, toward darkness and death, toward eros and embodiment.

I began to wonder about the earthy parts of the Last Supper, the smells and sounds, the feelings and fears. I let my imagination play with the story in the tradition of midrash, the Jewish practice of expansion and commentary on Scripture as paraphrase, prophecy, and parable. Each chapter of this book is really an earthy commentary on the central notion of embodiment and change — that we can trust the inward guidance of the soul *if* we pay attention to its expression in the world.

CLAY

Clay alerted me to the importance of body in the process of soul making. Potters commonly speak of clay as a "body" type. Another potter might ask me, "What clay body are you using?" to find out whether I am working with stoneware, porcelain, or earthenware clay. Not only is the clay itself referred to as "the body," but the words for parts of a clay vessel are body words: belly, shoulder, neck, and lip. So working with clay invited me to make connections between my spiritual life and the work of my hands, between Christ's body and my own.

Like our bodies, the clay body is important because its nature and consistency influence what the artist can make with it. Clay has a character to be reckoned with, a nature to be known and respected. In the beginning I worked with porcelain because that is what my mentor, Louie Mideke of Bellingham, Washington, used. It was smooth, strong, and kind to my hands. It seemed most suited to refined shapes, finished forms, and lovely glazes. Porcelain seemed especially suited to my growing sense of "the feminine" and gave form to my inner life. Because I had chosen a clay body that was quite different from the plain and pragmatic extrovert I seemed to be in public, I began to think of clay as the language of my soul.

CHANGE

Changing old patterns can be difficult if we operate with a mechanical or static model of reality and do not really believe that change is possible. But if we learn to read the signs of life all around us, and if we discover that we are indeed created to be creative, then we can rediscover the power and resourcefulness of imagination — another aspect of the soul. We can change patterns we have grown up with and come home to our bodies as a source of wisdom. We can help our souls find a mode of expression and trust the guidance we get from the inside. We can even learn the deep healing power of love and sexuality if we are not afraid to "get our hands dirty" in the every-dayness of soul work.

Clay was my teacher, and from the clay process I have drawn a model for change, but your expression might be handwork, housework, or some form of physical activity, which we often relegate to the category of recreation (i.e., re-creation). At the heart of re-creation is the process of change, of making a new start, of breaking old patterns and beginning new ones. Something more than setting goals and meeting them. I am speaking of internal change that results in a new form and shape in the physical world. That is the heart of this book: conscious, embodied change.

Each chapter begins with a description of a step in the process of turning clay into fired pottery, and connections to a model of change are highlighted.

First, the basic elements of clay itself suggest we have to be *grounded* by considering what is essential, basic, and necessary. Where do we start? What do we start with? What really matters?

Then, the act of *kneading* invites us to a position of readiness, of mixing the disparate parts to a point where change can happen.

Centering calls our focus and attention to particular possibilities and, at the same time, calls us to see them as a part of a greater whole.

Shaping lets our inner spirit force expand against the outer "givens," pulling, stretching, unbalancing options to try different choices, to see what happens, to see what fits.

Finishing pushes us to trust that change is not a one-time event, that we can stop and identify what we have created, and then let it go in order to make room for something new.

Glazing requires us to envision beyond what we can see and feel in the present, to claim something more than we know. Glazing reminds us of the capacity for play and decoration, the courage to risk and amplify what we have started. To become more and more who we are, not who someone else envisions.

And, finally, *firing* requires commitment and trust in transformation. We are reminded not to be impatient, to look forward and not be afraid of who we are becoming, to trust that we can be tried by fire and emerge in new ways.

STORIES

The voices of biblical women have been my companions on the way because my own spiritual tradition was shaped by the Church. My grandmother told me Bible stories long before I could read. I learned from her to think of God as a loving parent and Jesus as a friend. But, as an adult, conscious of my woman's body, I began to search for the stories of women who moved beyond a parental God to wrestle with the ramifications of uncertainty and even chaos in the world where no loving parent will save us from distress. These women of the Bible have taught me how to be more than a child of God. They have shown me what it means to be an adult of God, living with uncertainty and mystery.

Their stories are not commonly heard in church — at least not twenty-five years ago, when I started to look with my soul. So I have included the voices of two biblical women in each chapter because what they have to say might be a surprise to you, too. Most of these women have been overlooked by traditional interpreters of Scripture, but their stories are signs for women who walk the way of soul making. The monologues can be used as dramatic readings for a group meeting, followed by discussion in small groups of the journal questions.

My personal "communion" stories are included as an invitation for you to see your own life as a dialogue with the Divine. I believe our souls seek expression, and we each have the creative power to find that language or form. As we tell our stories, we become creators. And then the word that became flesh in our flesh can be offered to others, which will empower us with hope for the future.

JOURNAL QUESTIONS

Following each of the main sections, there are journal questions for you to use alone or with a small group. All of the journal questions can be shared (in dyads or triads to allow enough time for each person to be heard), but I have also included a special "group question" in each section to encourage you to create something together as an expression of your common purpose and companionship.

Consider other women you might want to gather with you as you read and study this book. Take time at your first meeting to formulate some guidelines for your time together (no advice or cross-talk, each person has a turn, all sharing is held in confidence, etc.). Select someone to be responsible each week for convening the group and bringing supplies. Decide at the first meeting how you want to start and end each session.

Until I started working with clay, I had always thought of community as the place one lived and worked. A neighborhood or a town. Maybe a church. Although the community created by my pots was more scattered, less coherent, yet I sensed that this community shared some common values that were closely related to the earth, both literally and figuratively. From my customers I learned that questions are an invitation to exchange, to mutual vulnerability out of which caring can emerge. The group questions in each chapter are designed to help you move from getting acquainted to deepening your experience together as a community.

◆

In a day when cynicism and despair hover just below bright smiles and aching hearts, I want to encourage you to take your own humanity seriously. We are already spiritual beings. The task that Jesus came to teach his friends was how to be fully human — loving deeply and enjoying our creativity to heal the wounded, feed the hungry, and release the prisoners in every household, neighborhood, and city. I long for the changes that could happen if we release our souls to imagine a better future for ourselves and our children.

"This is My Body..."

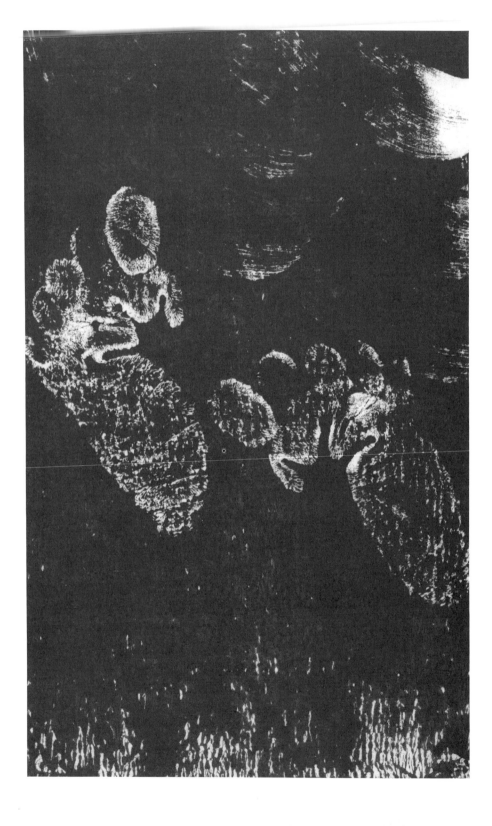

Chapter 1

GROUNDING

STARTING WITH THE
BASIC ELEMENTS

Stone and water dance together,
grinding one rock against another
into microscopic particles.
The tiny platelets are washed farther
and farther away from their source
until they find a pool and grow still.
There they sink to mix
with decaying plants and animals —
the organic slime that will become clay,
pliable and able to hold a shape.

CHILDREN EVERYWHERE reach for the mud in creek beds or roadside puddles, to squish out a shape and delight in what their own hands have made. At some level, we are all born to be artisans, to create and change. Our souls long for expression in the physical world. We are, even in this sophisticated age, tool-makers and artists who make objects for the sheer joy of personal expression. What we instinctively knew as children we have to reclaim intentionally if we are to keep our humanity in the midst of change, whether that change is self-generated or created by external circumstances.

Working with clay has brought me back to the primal link between my soul and the cycles of change and creativity in nature. Made of stone, water, and organic slime, clay is the elemental mixture found everywhere in the world, off-spring of the earth itself. When I work with clay and ground myself in the elements of nature, I feel like I am coming home to the earth after a long time away, having been lost in a world of words and concepts. Working with clay wakes me up, calls me back to my senses, and gives my soul a tangible expression, a language with shape and size.

STONE: PHYSICAL BODY

Clay begins as stone pushed up through the earth's crust by volcanic action or pressed down into layers and meta-morphosed by pressure. Because the stony sources differ, each clay "body" has its own distinctive color and smell, texture and toughness. Like us, clay is common everywhere in the world and yet unique to its origins. Each type of clay has its own "family tree" made of its particular combination of the three basic elements.

Just as each clay body is characterized by its stone source, we, too, begin with our basic body elements, the bone and flesh we were born with. Knowing our beginnings, our ground, is an essential prelude to initiating change. We need to know who we are, to accept the "givens" of physical body and past history, and to identify what makes us unique. Are we lean, wiry, and quick? Large-boned and laconic? What family characteristics dictate the strength and energy levels that we bring to the process of change? And what does our choice of expression say about our soul's source?

When I began working with clay in 1965, I wanted a compatible clay body to complement my strength and energy. I searched for a clay that would not chew at my hands with splintering sharpness, and I finally settled on porcelain, a dense, smooth, high-firing clay native to Asian highlands and manufactured from local sources in the United States. In retrospect, my choice of clay was probably more than a physical match of the clay body to my body: It was an expression of my soul's need for beauty and strength, the physical and metaphysical combined.

WATER: RELATIONSHIPS

The relationship between water and stone is essential to the formation of clay. Without water, clay would not come to be. We, too, are dependent on a flowing stream of relationships, our community, to give us form. Just as water moves, wears, and tames the stone, our relationships shape and smooth us over time. Washing clarifies and defines the basic ingredients by sorting the clay particles while they are being washed far from their origins. Without our "watery feelings" of tears and laughter, the full range of human relationships do not develop. Streams and rivers — like human institutions of marriage, family, friends, community — make a natural sluice, catching the heavier particles in stone baffles while carrying lighter layers farther on, sifting them in the process. Finally, what is left is fine and free of rocks, laid down layer upon layer wherever water pools.

Moving water and still water have different functions in making clay. Moving water tears down and refines, while pooled water allows collection, expansion, and internal change. Still water holds the stone while other processes happen, just as the womb holds, rocks, and feeds us while we are growing inside for nine months. In that primary relationship, uterine waters nourish and remove waste from the fetus without effort from the mother or the water-breathing child: the relationship just *is*. This watery world before birth is the primary communion that we have all experienced — with God and with another human being. Gestation is Eden experienced and held in our cells as an ancient memory when birth casts us out onto land and requires breath for survival. Our first creative act is to draw a deep breath of air!

SLIME: WORK

Although weathered stone and moving water are the basic elements from which clay is formed, without the addition of death and decay, clay could not be shaped or molded. Waste has a purpose in nature. Organic slime makes clay slippery and coherent, recycling natural waste to make the stony mix into a sticky mass. Water welcomes death and actively assists decomposition, forming a gelatinous substance that gradually bonds with the clay molecules. Over time, natural decay makes the clay "plastic" and moldable so the micro-scopic clay platelets can slide past one another.

Making body waste is probably a child's first work, her first "production." Elimination is part of a dynamic natural order in which growing and dying is always present; a child's bowel movement is a sign of health. As a child matures, she produces other things: art projects, stories, order or chaos in her space — precursors to her later work in the world. Just as decay is recycled as pliability in clay, nourishment in the form of air, food, and love goes into the body, and waste comes out to be recycled by the earth: Exhaled air is used by plants, food becomes fertilizer, and love builds human community when it is given as well as received. Our purpose or work in the world joins with that of others in a living system of birth and death, of creativity and decay.

My understanding of the link between bodily waste production and work was a gift I received from the clay. I knew that decaying matter was essential for making clay workable, and this helped me see that our work is the natural product of who we are and how our bodies function in time and relationship with others in society. The question is one of balance or depletion of the whole complex system of individuals, communities, peoples, and the natural world. Organic slime reminds us that work is meant to make the community function more flexibly, with ease and elasticity. If organic slime makes the difference between fine sand and pliable clay, then we might examine our work for signs of spiritual health or illness. Is there a good balance between what we take in and what we produce? How does our work — whether paid or not — affect the pliability and potential re-formation of our community?

The clay's plasticity affects the kind of work a potter produces. As I experimented with different clays, I looked for one that would move well and be responsive to my touch. Some clay is "short," denied the glue of slippery decay, forever breaking into sandy bits instead of clinging to the shape that fingers make. By contrast, other clay has too much ooze and will not hold an upright shape. The porcelain clay I finally chose was an expression of my unique form of creativity, sturdy enough for everyday table use and refined enough for experiments with color and decoration. Starting with the particular combination of stone, water, and slime that characterizes porcelain was the grounding I needed to find a form for my creative urge. Porcelain became the language of my soul.

Journal Questions

1. Look around the place where you are right now and identify an object to symbolize yourself. Describe the object in your journal. How does your description connect with your body?
2. Choose some other object to represent one primary relationship (a family member or close friend). Briefly describe that relationship.
3. Now look in your wallet (or imagine what is in it) for a symbol of your work, whether or not that is a paid job. How does that symbol connect with your work?

GROUP: Select a cloth for grounding your symbols in the center of your group and add any other symbols of your hopes for this time together. Talk together about some simple ceremony for beginning and ending each session (e.g., light a candle, pray in a circle, sing a familiar song, take a few minutes of silence.)

GROUNDING STORIES: BIBLICAL WOMEN

When I think of women's stories from the Judeo-Christian tradition in light of my experience with clay, I am drawn naturally to the first women in each testament for grounding stories: first Eve, then Mary.

When we listen to Eve's story, we hear of her grounding in her body, her relationships, and her work as Mother of All the Living (the meaning of her name). She calls us away from the terrible burden of being good to the joy of mutual love and exploration. When we hear Mary's grounding story, we hear the hopes and fears of a young woman who took her body seriously as a sacred gift. Mary struggled in her

closest relationships to accept the strangeness of God's way
of bringing a divine child into the world of substance. She
finally had to release the very body of Jesus to find her own
work among the disciples.

EVE'S STORY
(Genesis 2-3; 4:1-2; 5:1-4)

In the beginning God was creating all things,
blowing spirit into fleshy forms,
making animals, birds, and fish.
Finally, God shaped a human form
from the dust of the earth
(so the story goes),
body and head, two legs, two arms,
two hands for making things —
but it had neither laughter nor tears,
at first.

God blew the breath of being into the clay
(so the story goes)
and set the being in a garden
with all kinds of trees and flowers,
birds and fish and animals.
None were like the human one,
and so
it was
alone.

Time passed.
The clay dried and then a crack appeared
(so the story goes).

And out of the crack, soft clay came.
Then God fashioned two different beings
from the heart like stone,
one male and the other female.
God breathed a living soul into each of us.

Adam got his name from the red river clay,
which we call "adamah."
My name is Eve: "Mother of All the Living."

We were meant to be partners,
naked to one another,
not hiding or ashamed of our bodies,
because our creation as male and female
was good in God's eye.

God knew about good and evil,
about separating things into categories,
and told us we should not eat the fruit
of the Tree of the Knowledge of Good and Evil,
nor of the Tree of Life,
though both trees were left in the garden
where we were naked and unknowing innocents.
God said we would die if we ate of those trees,
but the wise serpent said we would not die.

I wondered what this dying was.
Time took its toll on living things,
but plants revived each spring.
The serpent shed its skin as newness came.
What sort of death would be a threat
beyond this cycle we could already see?

Could God have forgotten
that we couldn't divide things
into right and wrong yet?
We didn't understand the difference
between what we should and shouldn't do.

Like a little child (I later learned),
I explored everything by taste and touch —
the hard and soft, bitter and sweet —
learning all the while.
At last I came to the forbidden trees
and knew not what this dying was.
We ate of the Tree of the Knowledge of Good and Evil
and then understood
what God was talking about.

"Yes" and "No" became clear.
We learned of right and wrong,
understood the categories called good and evil.
After eating the fruit, we knew we had done wrong,
so we hid.

When God came walking in the garden
in the cool of the evening,
calling for us to come and talk,
we felt ashamed.
We could see ourselves from outside,
from God's eyes instead of our own.
Becoming conscious, we called it later
when we tried to tell the story
of what had happened.

"Now you have become like one of us," God said,
sighing slightly like the wind,
"but you must live the cycles of the earth
while at home in body form and substance."

Then God sent us out of the garden
with a mark on each of us
to show that we were made in God's image
and not to be killed for food.
Sent out like silt in a river
to be tumbled and sifted by the difficulties of life.

We learned to laugh and cry,
to claim our humanness
and teach our little ones
to love instead of fear.
That became our most important work.

The little ones.
Only three were named
when writing was introduced during David's reign:
Cain, Abel, and Seth.
But we had other sons and daughters, too.
Male and female, made to mate and create,
to feel joy and sorrow,
to know right and wrong
in relationships.

As Adam and I grew older,
we knew death could not be far in the future.
We had seen animals age and die,

knew it was God's way to keep the earth
renewed.

I see it now.
It is no sin to die.
Our shame and hiding came from consciousness,
from knowing how to name things good and evil.
But grounding life again in God's creative hand
has made our love
the lasting part
of body life.

We must let go
and sink into the earth,
like clay in its great cycle of
stone, water, and slime,
back to the source again.

Journal Questions

1. *Where did your name come from? What associations do you have with your name?*
2. *Recall a childhood incident of breaking the rules. If or when you were caught, how did you feel? What did you learn?*
3. *Write your own "creation myth" about your birth.*

GROUP: Let those who are willing read their creation myths aloud. How do you feel about hearing and telling those beginning stories?

MARY'S STORY
(Luke 1-2; 8:19-21; Matthew 13:55; Mark 6:3;
John 2:1-12; 19:25-27; Acts 1:14)

As a child, my parents were utterly important,
and what they said, I did.
They taught me right and wrong,
good and bad, the Law and the prophets.
They were my source and strength.
As a child, I was grounded in our family, clan, and people.
As a Jew, I knew I was a child of God.

Now I am a Virgin,
bleeding monthly and able to bear a child.
I know my sacred power now.
Unashamed of my nakedness,
I can dedicate my life to God
instead of to what my parents want.

I ponder many thoughts inside
— the source of life
— the why of bodies
— and being female.
I think of Eve
as Mother of All the Living,
even me.

At night, I speak to her
because the mystery of her body
is entwined with mine.
I breathe the water of her womb
in all my dreams.
But my wonderings do not last long.

◆

One night an angel came crashing in to my quietness
to tell me I had conceived and would bear a son!
"How can it be?" I said, surprised,
"for I have no husband!"
I know where babies come from!
The women have revealed these things to me
as we meet apart,
secluded from daily activities during our moon cycles.
We tell stories of creation,
of Adam and Eve,
how clay and living spirit — adamah and spiritus —
must meet and mate to make another soul.
"How can it be?"

But the brightness from God assured me it was so.
Told me a manchild would be shaped in my womb,
known by God before his bones were knit together . . .
known by me, fed by my body, too,
before his organs formed.
My body,
the sacred temple where the miracle of birth takes place!
From Virgin to Vessel, grounded in God!

◆

If I'm pregnant, I must flee.
Men's rules.
The people who think they know of good and evil
will not believe I have been faithful to Joseph.
They could kill both me and the child.

Oh, Mother Eve, help me carry this earthly child safely
to his birth and beyond.
Help me be his watery home,
his River of Life.
Let my body be the basket in which he safely rocks,
like Moses, who was sheltered from death
until placed in a home that was safe from harm.
Help me make my own exodus journey safely,
to the hill country where Elizabeth lives.

If the angel is right,
this child will be trouble for others,
his body a barrier and blessing
to those who want God to be only spirit.

Oh, Mother Eve, help me to flow with the changes ahead,
to drop what I do not need to carry
and even welcome death should it come,
so I may know the fullness of my being,
my purpose, my call.

Let me live to see the future of this child,
to be shaped and molded inside and out
until at last it is time for me
to pass through the fires
of purification,
returning me to the Source
from whence this child has come.

Oh, Mother Eve, stay with me now
as I make the passage from Virgin to Mother
without the comfort and protection of a husband.

You come to me as Elizabeth,
whose wise, wrinkled face
helps me remember the angel's word.
Her body makes it real.
Soon mine will swell with child,
and I will see the Spirit take on flesh
in me.
Be with me now, I pray.

Journal Questions

1. As an adolescent, what were some of your hopes and fears associated with your body?
2. When and how did you "leave home" as a young adult?
3. What were some of your dreams and fears for the future as you left home? Did you have a special friend then? How was this friend important to you?

GROUP: Sitting in a circle, tell each other one special "leaving home" story.

RECONNECTING WITH THE EARTH

If starting with the basic elements of life is the first step in choosing to change, for me that means reconnecting with the earth itself. The cycles of nature remind me not to be afraid of death or endings, to expect new life to come out of waste and decay. My own story of learning to let go of fear begins with a trip to a place where I had seen a vein of clay exposed.

Ground squishes between my toes,
coating my feet in blue
as earthy smells surround me walking on the beach.
The clay holds my footprint,
cupping water, then sand, from lapping waves.
My feet have found what I came for:
a vein of clay, tipped and held compressed for eons,
now exposed by a creek running into Puget Sound.
I stop to dig,
noting how far I will have to carry the gunnysack
back to my car.

The clay body is heavy and dense with sea water,
smooth as skin.
I dig carefully, avoiding shells and stones.
The texture is slick, and it smells full of rich nutrients.
I let my mind traverse the years back to a time
when this clay was just a layer of sediment on the beach.
As I work, shoveling clay into a sack,
my body bows to our common source
long before I was born.

My wondering takes me beyond space and time,
but my feet stay firmly grounded in the present,
my toes feeling for danger.
Spirit dancing with substance creates a soul connection
as I play kairos with the time of then and now.

"Meditate on your being the moment before conception,"
I remember hearing.
So I do.

And see only darkness.
No squiggling sperm or large permeable egg
comes to my mind's eye,
but pulsing darkness like the sea:
the soul's source,
the universal heart.
Is that you, God?

As spirit became flesh in me,
my particular source stones were not alike:
mountain basalt as my father,
desert sandstone as mother.
Genes pulled from their sperm and egg
mysteriously knew when to make skin and bone,
coded by them, yes,
but still unique.
Playfully different.
Unlike my sisters.
Where does that uniqueness come from?

A deeper source breaks in,
refusing the limit of genealogy.
What fire formed the first stone?
What water bore the makings of my soul?
First no-thing was there, then some-thing was.
Birthed by the heart of God, the poets say.

Then back to my body again.
Water-rocked in my mother's body . . .
fed by her blood and breath
until a pool of pure clay

settles into form and
makes my body me.

Her body died a little to give mine life.
Teeth softened.
Muscles sagged as the child was formed in living water.
Moving molecules clung together,
making each of my members
according to an ancient plan
passed on from generation to generation —
the gift of death to life and back again in my own body.
Water welcomes death back to the earth,
recycles everything that is not toxic
to its changing powers.

But death does not feel benign to me,
this child left by those who mattered most.
Dad was sent "overseas" for war.
Mother "took a rest cure" in a TB sanitarium
while he was gone.
Her fear was full of death
because her mother was the sole survivor of six sisters:
All died of tuberculosis as young adults.
Dad's mother took us in.

Left behind
to sink and form again.
Too bad to take along, I thought.
Fearful that Grandma might get mad and lock us out.
Always conscious we must be good.
Bonded to my sister in tight embrace

to keep away my fears at night:
the war, a hard dry spot
in the green grass grounding of my inner child.
Revisited when, a generation later,
my husband, Peter, went two different times to Vietnam.
While he was gone, I learned to work with clay
to salve my soul.
I didn't know the clay would give me
language for my grief,
giving form to newness as I wept.

As though stored in the earth
until I was ready to know what I already knew,
clay opened the door to memory for me.

While my hands worked,
my mind had blank time
to wander though abandoned rooms,
lost caves of childhood.
Early experience took on form and substance in time again,
moving from past to present, enriching my inner life —
just when I felt impoverished by Peter's absence.

Clay continued when he returned,
becoming the language of love.
Male and female in elemental mix.

"This is my body . . ." we say to each other
by touch and by word.
Like two stones, wearing each other smooth over time,
we tumble our I-ness against each other

in the river from our beginnings,
making a moldable mass of I and we,
of us and me.
Still learning to love after thirty years together.
Today there are also others
who teach me how to love and let go of what I make
to receive the new
that comes.

I feel grounded in the larger, longer cycles of the earth
as clay is made for future generations.
I know it now.
My grounding has three parts:
my body,
close relationships,
and my work in the world —
a sense of being in the right place
as I walk barefoot through my life,
testing each step with my toes.

Journal Questions

1. Find several "stones" or symbols to tell of the major
   turning points in your life. Describe or draw these in your
   journal.
2. What major events have "weathered" your life?
3. Where do you feel grounded today?

GROUP: Pair up and mold your partner as though she were
clay (for example, place her feet and arms in a certain
position). Then be the receiver, as though you were clay. Take
some time to discuss this experience with your partner.

GROUNDING AS COMMUNION

(Matthew 26:17-30; Mark 14:12-26; Luke 22:7-23; John 13:1-17)

Working with clay brought me back to the biblical account of the Last Supper with fresh eyes. I began to see this ancient sacrament of bread and wine as the biblical equivalent of grounding with clay — taking a common and yet unique "body," setting it apart by circumstance and action, celebrating change in the context of God's ultimate creativity.

The Last Supper is religious in the deepest sense of the word: the Latin *re* meaning *again* and *ligio, to connect.* To reconnect with the source of life. For me, reconnecting with the source of life is the essential beginning place for choosing into change with freedom instead of fear of annihilation.

"This is my body, broken for you," Jesus said to his gathered friends at Passover. *"Do this in remembrance of me."* I recognize in the familiar words of the sacrament a verbal expression of what my soul has found in the pottery studio: a way to express the union of my body and spirit in tangible form, to find language and form for the mystery of connectedness, and to claim my uniqueness.

I suspect that when we do not find the form of expression that is particularly appropriate to the clay mixture of our lives, violence or disease erupt out of the frustration. When we do find an expression — as Jesus did in revisioning Passover — we can deal with pain and death as part of God's larger, creative purpose. The ancient ritual of the Last Supper expands our contemporary understanding of ways to embrace unwanted or fearful change.

Grounding ourselves in the reality of being embodied is part of the Eucharist or Communion celebration. We take food and put it into our mouths. Our tongues taste and our souls are nourished. We are invited to "re-member" by doing these things together — in common, in community.

We are invited to the Communion table to be empowered for change. We are invited to release the stone of physical experience, to let the water of relationships tumble and sort what we need to leave behind, and to notice the "glue" of caring for one another as the basic elements that bring elasticity, flexibility, and readiness for change — not as a threat but as promise.

Chapter 2

KNEADING

INVITING A SENSE OF READINESS

Preparing the clay
before it is put on a potter's wheel
means working it against a hard surface
to mix all parts of the clay into a uniform mass.
The potter scoops a handful of clay from a bag or bin
and begins by rolling it on a board or slab of plaster
to make a coherent lump.
Pressing down to stretch the clay outward
and then rocking back,
lifting and folding the clay inward on itself
. . . a rhythmic down-and-up motion begins.
Pivoting the clay slightly,
the basic press-and-pull motion is repeated many times
until the clay is thoroughly mixed.

BEFORE THE DAY'S WORK BEGINS, most people go through a morning ritual of some kind: getting up, stretching, brushing teeth, showering, shaving, checking the weather, drinking coffee, locating car keys, or something similar. This routine marks the transition between sleeping and waking, between the metaphysical realm of dream and image, and ordinary rational activity. Images of the past are gathered into the present, and a focus on *this* day, *this* particular time and place, begins to grow. Similarly, at the border between everyday actions and the soul work of clay, kneading is a ritual of readiness for changes ahead.

Although kneading is necessary to mix the clay into a uniform mass, no particular thought is required and no decisions have to be made. When I am kneading, my body and the clay body speak directly to one another; there is an invitation to intentional relationship and mutual creativity. The clay presents limits and possibilities, and I bring my intentions, intuition, and skill. The whole-body motion of kneading provides time and space, creating a sense of anticipation for whatever will be born on this particular day.

BODY RHYTHMS

Kneading literally takes me to my knees on the floor of my pottery studio. Using a large plywood board, I kneel at one edge, using my body weight to keep the board from moving. In that position my whole body rocks forward, blood humming toward the heels of my hands as I press the mass of clay onto the board. Rocking back, my fingertips guide the clay up and around into position to press it down again just to one side of the first press, allowing the table surface to stretch the clay with each downward motion. Soon a spiral forms at one end of the lump, showing me that the clay is a uniform thickness and texture. The spiral — like the sworl at the end of a conch shell — indicates that I am kneading the clay effectively, mixing it thoroughly.

When I pot, I begin the day by kneading all the clay I will use for the day's production of bowls and mugs. That means twenty minutes or so of this primal motion — rocking back and forth, working large, undefined lumps of clay into springy, pliable mounds like bowl-sized batches of bread dough. The work is hard, full-bodied, and routine. I sink into my body and let my whole self be present to the texture of the clay.

My hands and arms awaken first, feeling the toughness of the clay after it has been sitting in a block, bagged and ready. As I bend forward and press down, my lower back muscles stretch, and contracting stomach muscles vie with my knees for attention. Then arms, shoulders, and neck muscles join as my blood begins to move in time with my breathing. As I work out the stiff parts of the clay, my body becomes more pliable, ready to move. As effective as any yoga stretch, kneading brings my whole body to the present moment.

Not only do I press my weight against the clay, but the clay has its own way of pressing back, resisting my action, reminding me that the clay has its own substance and character. As my body speaks and the clay answers back with its texture and toughness, I learn to respect the nature of that batch of clay. I adjust my weight, speed, and pressure in response. The clay and I establish a dialogue, there on the floor, grunting and pushing in the morning stillness, like two wrestlers.

The motions of kneading take me back to early child-hood and link my body with countless generations of humans learning to crawl, stand, and finally walk and speak. Rocking on hands and knees is thought to stimulate the parts of the brain needed for internal organization of thought and speech. Reconnecting with such a primary center of self through my body motions, I recognize knead-ing as a ritual of gathering in the disparate parts of myself — plans, interruptions, dreams, stray bits of speech and song — bringing everything to a single point of concentra-tion as I move to the second and third batch of clay with my prayer-full routine.

Kneading the clay makes me aware of my *whole* body, humming with life. The rocking and pressing motion affects my digestion, as well as stretches my muscles. As I knead the clay, my body is kneading food. I become aware of food in my stomach and bowel, aware of the whole inner cycle of food and elimination: fullness and emptiness, expansion and contraction. Kneading makes me conscious of the transformative cycle that my body engages in so naturally, turning food into energy, eliminating waste, and creating new growth all the time.

Then my body motions begin to move my awareness from outside actions to inner rhythms, awakening my soul. Perhaps it is my posture as much as the motion that quickens my sense of being in a holy place. On my hands and knees, I am at prayer in my pottery studio — not a prayer of talking, but of listening, of readiness, of willingness to be molded. I feel both powerful and receptive, strong and humble, creative and willing to do whatever I need to do — a posture of readiness, close to the earth, grounded in the here and now. I am fully present in this time, this place, this experience.

BREATHING

As my body teaches me about prayer at the primal level of bone and blood, my posture requires a deeper kind of breathing. Shallow breathing from the upper chest is not enough. Rocking forward forces the old air out of my lower lungs, and my whole body fills naturally as I rock back on my heels. The motion is a meditation practice — eyes open, body engaged, breathing synchronized and deep. Like doing CPR on myself, my breathing brings new life to my blood and brain, filling me with air and releasing tensions — bringing all of me to relaxed attentiveness.

I become aware of chronic tightness in my chest and throat, holding my voice as though in readiness for a critical question, but kneading cannot be sustained with such constriction. I learn to breathe as a baby does, letting my body fill and empty with a naturalness that brings relaxation and alertness. What a surprising discovery: I did not know how to breathe fully! Now the clay teaches me to breathe again and, in the breathing, how to be conscious of my aliveness. Eastern mystics know that the breath is a pathway to all that is holy, but we Westerners talk more about lung capacity and endurance than enlightenment through our breathing. As I knead the clay, it teaches me to be present and fully awake in the moment, to BE in the doing.

SILENCE

It was in 1968, when we moved to Hanover, New Hampshire, that I converted a bedroom into my first pottery studio. As I worked more deeply into my commitment to clay, I began to be aware of an inward shift toward a new place of stillness. At first, when I went to my studio with a cup of morning coffee, my thoughts running wildly ahead of my hands to plan my day's work, I would reach for the radio knob and let someone else's choice of music fill the air. We all do it: absent-mindedly filling space because we live in a world surrounded by sound. It is habit. We have been conditioned to choose a station and let someone else provide the programming.

Advertisers know that we are more susceptible when we are only half listening. They compete for our wake-up time. Radio alarms pour sound into the sleepy ear of the unconscious, shortening our dream time and filling the natural holy space of sleep with commands to hurry, with news of disasters and the latest scandal guaranteed to arouse our fears and suspicion before we are really awake. Sound is an easy addiction to have.

For some, sound is the comfort of having another presence there, no matter what the sound is. For me, the companionship of classical music seemed to elevate my thoughts and get me through the kneading time, which I assumed to be boring and routine in the beginning. But my body and the clay eventually quickened my consciousness and led me toward silence, one step at a time.

As I dropped into a state of meditation while kneading the day's clay, I began to notice the noise and, more importantly, to sense that my body's rhythm did not always fit with my favorite FM radio station. When I began throwing more difficult and unique pieces, I started to notice how the music distracted me. I would turn the radio off and let the studio be silent at those times. The silence helped me concentrate on the particulars of *this* shape, this moment, this part. I noticed subtleties I had missed previously. It was my first conscious connection with silence as a support for my creativity.

Finally, it dawned on me to keep the radio off as I began the day — to knead the clay in silence and be receptive, expecting, open. Using my whole body to stretch the clay against the worn board, I learned to watch the spiral flow out of my fingers. In silence, the simple repetitive actions of kneading and breathing together became an invitation to join a long line of potters back through history who had made simple vessels for the community they lived in. Kneading became the focus of my morning prayers, my act of obedience and willingness to learn what the clay had to teach me of silence.

INNER SOUNDS

Stillness brought with it a new kind of hearing. Without knowing that I was listening for something deeper, I began to hear inner voices that had been drowned out by the radio, some encouraging and some critical. Often I would begin the day with eagerness and expectation, the motion of kneading massaging a magical womb of images and ideas, ready for birth into form. I could hear joy in my body at a deep, internal level of spiritual creativity. At other times, my mind was blank. Nothing appeared. Then an accusing voice would begin: "See? You can't do this. Potting is a waste of time. And money. You'll never be good enough to make a living like this! What did we send you to college for anyway! Etc., etc. . . ."

But I discovered another voice, too. Quieter. Pulsing. Closer to my heart. Seemingly tidal, like the sound heard in a conch shell. Blood rhythms resounding in a quiet chamber. "The Encourager," I came to call that voice, from the French for heart, *le Coeur*. Courage. In the silence The Encourager whispered, "Be a beginner. Give yourself time. Let your hands learn. Your body knows the way. Relax. Listen. Practice." I began to trust that voice of my heart and to move away from the shrill critics that I carried from years of academic striving. I began letting my breath take me deeper into a dialogue with the clay, allowing myself to be a learner, and thus a beginner, again and again.

In the daily quiet of my pottery studio, I began to trust The Encourager. Mistakes mattered less and less. I could always rework the clay and start again. To punish myself for not already knowing how to make a particular shape was to short-circuit the process of learning. Kneading included reworking clay that had been used on the wheel, redeeming it for another round. I began to understand forgiveness as the process of letting go of one thing in order to focus on another. Gradually, I realized that kneading was not simply a task I had to do before the real work of potting could begin. Instead, kneading was the centerpoint, the ritual of bringing my self to the clay as a pilgrim, a seeker.

My stance shifted from being the director and controller to being the listener and learner. I became more attentive to the nature of the clay itself, as well as to the process of kneading, and later, to throwing it on the wheel. The clay seemed to be calling me to something more, something bigger than I could think about with the words I already knew. From the silence I had chosen, I moved to a quieter place inside. The squirrel cage of busy thoughts began to slow and then to stop (occasionally) as my body worked in known and familiar patterns. I learned to love the ordinary routine of opening a box of clay, slicing off a large block, and beginning to feel its particular texture and tone. The routines of preparation became a birthing process for me as well as the clay.

As kneading took me deeper into the present moment, I could hear the inner sounds of deeper guidance where boundaries between inner life and outer work diffuse become more permeable. *This* is who I am, here and now, not what others have told me in the past. This is what I have to work with, not some other energy or skill. I began to feel at home in the present moment, collected and engaged, not simply waiting for something in the future. "This is my body" began to make more sense to me. I realized that kneading had become body prayer.

Journal Questions

1. *What is your routine in the morning? How is it a ritual of readiness for your day?*
2. *What body motions help you breathe fully and deeply? What happens when you breathe and become aware of yourself?*
3. *When are the times of quiet in your day? If you would like more, when would that be? How might you experiment with silence?*
4. *Write down a few phrases that your inner critic says to you. If you had an inner voice of encouragement, what would it say to you?*

GROUP: *Sitting in a circle, speak the encouraging messages you would like to hear. Listen carefully and note any that seem especially important for you.*

KNEADING STORIES: BIBLICAL WOMEN

Miriam, sister of Moses, and Elizabeth, cousin to Mary, lived their kneading stories, their body-prayers, at the border between physical and divine presence. For Miriam, who shared leadership during the Hebrew's exodus from Egypt, kneading marked the cultural shift of her people from idol-worship in Egypt to the mysterious "I AM" God beyond all others. For Elizabeth, kneading was the gestation period when she and Mary were each pregnant with a new future for their people, she with John, Mary with Jesus. Past and present were gathered in their friendship. Elizabeth's child "leaped for joy" in the womb in recognition of Mary's unborn child, confirming that *this* was the one they had been waiting for. *This* child, *this* mother.

MIRIAM'S STORY
(*Exodus 2:1-10; 15:19-21; Numbers 12; 20:1-2;*
Deuteronomy 24:8-9; I Chronicles 6:1-3; Micah 6:3-4)

"Don't move, Miriam.
Keep watch over your little brother.
His life depends on you."

That's the voice of my mother, whispering . . .
Long before light came to the river,
we were here with the basket among the reeds.

"Be very still. Keep your breathing quiet.
If Moses wakes up, feed him this.
The water will rock him, soothe him . . .
You won't have to wait long.
The princess comes early to bathe."

So I wait, going over the plans we have made.
Pharaoh's daughter wants a son
to assure her a place of succession.
Would she take a Hebrew child?
A child who would be known by his circumcision?

Perhaps. She's a rebel.
It's our only chance to save Moses.
Every male child is to be killed,
and he is growing too big to hide.

My feet are getting numb.
I try not to move, except my toes.
Suppose I can't move when they come . . .

I go over my mother's words one more time:
"Watch for the Pharaoh's daughter.
She comes here to bathe.
Let them discover the basket, the baby.
That's the critical moment.
Move quickly then.
Speak directly to her, not to one of the other women.
Tell her you can find a wet nurse.
Don't be afraid, Miriam.
I know God will protect you and give you the words."

So I wait,
quiet as a stone,
praying I'll know what to do, how to be,
hearing her speak in my heart.
Body. Breath. Silence. Words.
Waiting while Moses rocks in the reeds.

Pharaoh has forbidden men to come here,
where the princess bathes.
I have nothing to fear . . . until she comes.
I must not drift off.
I must stay awake. Stay alert. Breathe.
Listen to my heart.
Speak the words God will give me to save Moses.

Holy Mother, stay with me . . .

◆

Now, those hours by the river seem long ago.
Preparation, really, for what was to come.

Discipline. Teaching me to wait and watch.
Teaching me when to act, too.
Teaching me to listen for my inner voice.

Now I'm known as a prophet,
one who speaks for God.
Aaron, Moses, and I
interpret signs of God
when the people need a face
instead of smoke by day or fire by night.
We've come a long way from the riversong in my heart.

First, there was Moses and his rage.
Living with the slurs and slander of the court.
Always feeling less than the others.
Knowing his people were slaves,
even though the Pharaoh treated him like a son.

Then Moses' anger spilled out against a soldier.
Seen by our people, known, rejected.
Had to flee.
We didn't know where for a long time,
but I knew he was in God's hand.
Heard it, inside my heart.
Knew God in my prayers.
Discovered God in my waiting.

Now Moses is grown
and married to Zipporah from Midian,
whose father is a priest.
He will have children, but I will not.

My role is different: virgin and prophet.
A woman unto herself.
My children will have to be God's people.
My family, the one I was born to.
My God, the guide in my heart.

Moses speaks of God's voice in the burning bush!
I heard it long before, as I stood by the river.
I heard the whisper in the reeds,
helping me stay with my task,
letting me know what to do, what to say, when to move.

Moses speaks of the bush,
of God's command to confront the Pharaoh,
and his own fears of rejection —
not so much by Pharaoh as by our people.
Would they accept his leadership?
Yahweh answered so clearly,
"Tell them I AM sent you."

My task was small by comparison . . .
just to watch over one child.
The I AM in me helped me stay.
"I AM the soul of your people," I heard in the rushes,
as the water curled about my thighs.
"I AM with you always."

Moses had to face the Pharaoh;
I had only to face my fears.
But I know God was with us both.

We danced to I AM
when the Red Sea closed over our enemies,
drowning them all.
"Miriam's dance," they called it
because I was the one who knew
we needed to stop and celebrate.
The sea gave birth to us, as a people.
So we danced! I danced!
Our soul was born that day!
God came alive in our midst,
melding us together.

Later on, when Moses was gone from us for so long,
Aaron and I argued about making an image.
The people were restless.
Some began packing to go back.
"Why did you bring us here to starve?" they cried,
and I could not find enough silence to hear God's voice.

"If only I could find water," I thought to myself,
"I would know what to do."
I would stand in the silence
and let the water whisper encouragement.
But there was no water,
no place to stand and hear God's voice
in the stillness of the reeds.

So we melted our jewelry and made a golden calf,
there in the desert.
The people needed something they could see and touch.

Aaron and I were not able to convince them
of God's presence — God's promise:
"I AM with you always."

Moses was furious!
Sent the tablets crashing to the ground,
breaking them into a million pieces,
turning them into stone again.
Clay tablets, fired by the face of God, he said.

I was terrified!
Would we all be killed?
Would God turn from us?
Leave us in the desert?

No, God was kneading us like clay.
Pushing us against our old habits of worshipping idols.
Freeing us from the past.
Preparing us for the future.
Making us one body, one soul.

Aaron and I were changed from the inside out,
as Moses must have been earlier —
when he was seared by the heat of the bush.
We felt the fire of God's anger
at the idol we had made of gold.
All three of us were changed!

From then on, I could hear the voice of I AM
in the silence.
Encouraging me. Guiding us.

I heard it then and I hear it now,
not all the time, but strong and clear when it counts.
This way and not that.

Pushing us. Pressing us
into readiness.
Where I AM leads, we will go.

"Our prophets," they call us,
Aaron, Moses, and me.

Journal Questions

1. Where in your life do you "stand and wait" for others?
2. When and how has being an "elder sister" helped you or hurt you?
3. Describe a time when you danced with glee or celebrated a victory.

GROUP: Stand and close your eyes. Let your body express how you feel about this group. Talk together about expressing your feelings with your body. Then close your eyes and move your body into a gesture of thanks for the Guiding Spirit of this group.

ELIZABETH'S STORY
(Luke 1)

My body has been an empty vessel, ready to hold a child
but not filled by the favor of God.
Though he wanted a son,
Zachariah did not choose another wife,
as he might have.

Perhaps he, too, was still praying.
We never talk about it any more,
for we are old, he and I,
used to each other like worn sandals
shaped by the path we have walked together.

We both come from Aaron's line.
Powerful and prophetic.
Blessed as priests in the house of God.
I even carry the name of Aaron's wife,
but nothing helped me conceive the child
I so dearly wanted.

Then one day Zachariah came home from the temple,
and he could not speak!
Struck dumb, though he could walk perfectly well.
He wrote three words in the dust:
"angel . . . baby . . . you."
Just those. I was speechless!
Could he have seen an angel?
Was a baby promised? At our old age?

I could not believe it.
And yet I did.
I had never stopped praying for a child.
Could see him, perfect, blessed by God.
A special child. Our son.

I stopped going to the market every day
because I was almost afraid to hope.
Needed to wait until the babe quickened to life.

I didn't want to face the gossip.
Suppose I was wrong.
Deluded. A crazy old woman.

As it was, everyone knew that Zachariah could not speak.
He was a priest, used to speaking in public.
A stroke, they said.
So people felt sorry for us and brought us food.
We stayed close to home, waiting.

During those months of solitude,
my body felt different, alive, changing inside.
I could almost feel a child growing there in silence,
but I have been disappointed before.
So I kept praying and working and waiting,
knowing nine months would eventually pass.

We both lived in silence.
Zachariah studying, walking,
not going to the temple
for the usual arguments with other priests.
I kept to myself,
not going to the well with the other women.
They were too full of questions.

I could hardly believe what was happening inside.
My heart sang to God all day and night.
Think of it! Me! A mother at last!

As my body began to change, grow big,
my mind was flooded with images.

One night I saw an angel, as clear as day,
speaking to my cousin Mary.
She was terribly afraid . . . as I had been.
But she had more reason.
(Well, maybe not. . . .
Birth is a threat for someone as old as I am.)
But she is so young and not married yet to Joseph.
The angel told her not to be afraid,
told her that she would bear a son — a very special son.
The Messiah!
The one we've all been waiting for.

Then Mary came to visit me, and I knew it was true!
My baby jumped. I felt life for the first time.
Filled with life and light and love.
The Holy Spirit came,
and I knew we were on holy ground.

Mary and I had a wonderful time
in the three months she was here.
What a pair we were!
An old woman and a young teen-ager.
She was quick and lively, but still afraid.
I was slow and heavy,
but sure that God would bless us both
with strength to hold whatever lay ahead
for our two sons.

Of course I felt safer than Mary:
I was married to Zachariah,
I'd been wanting a child for so long.

Mary was almost a child herself.
So I had to keep reminding her who she was —
chosen by God.

"Mary, Mary," I would say to her in the evenings
when we would sit together and I would brush her hair,
"remember who you are."

Such help she was that I hated to see her go,
but she left after my babe was born.
The neighbors thought he would be named
after his father,
but the angel I talked to so often inside my heart
said he was to be called John ("God is gracious").
We knew that was right
when writing his name — John —
gave Zachariah his speech again,
unlocked his lips and let the sound come out.

Mary's fresh young face came back to me
many times after she left,
so eager and questioning,
like the future itself.

And she told me later that my words gave her courage
and strength to go back to Nazareth,
where she waited for her child to be born.

"Remember who you are," she would repeat to herself.
I guess I did say that to her, by way of encouragement.
Funny, what we give each other from the heart.

Journal Questions

1. *Can you remember a time when a friend came to share a waiting time with you or helped you live into a change? Describe or color your experience.*
2. *What special qualities of your friend were important to you?*
3. *Imagine your friend saying to you, " [your name] , remember who you are." What do those words mean to you?*

GROUP: Pair up and say to your partner, "_____, remember who you are," three times. Then pause and hear those words from your partner. Then talk about the experience.

READINESS FOR GOD'S PRESENCE

Kneading clay led me toward a new experience of worship and changed my understanding of church from a place of *answers* to a place of *readiness* for God's presence. In 1969, when my husband was in Vietnam for the second time, I felt unable to pray in traditional ways. When I sat in a church pew, trying so hard to find a sense of inner peace, I felt incapable of reaching the same level of focus I experienced while kneading clay in my pottery studio. I soon noticed that I was holding my breath during worship, as though I was waiting for something to happen inside. I could not quiet my thoughts or turn off the anxious voices that were playing as loud as any radio in my head.

Someone suggested I try an early morning Eucharist service, which our pastor celebrated for his own preparation. I found it was the form of worship I had been missing. The body motion of kneeling at the Communion rail opened the channel I was seeking. The small chapel was filled with ladder-back chairs, and no one kneeled (as we might have in an Episcopal church with kneeling benches) until we gathered at the rail to receive the elements of bread and wine. But when I felt the hardness of the floor through that little cushion and leaned forward, cupping my hands to receive the bread, I was ready: "This is my body, broken for you," the pastor would say, placing a small piece of bread in my hands. "Do this in remembrance of me."

My body, kneeling there at the rail, was finally ready to receive the bread as real food for my soul. My breathing slowed, deepened, filled my belly with air and lifted away the fear I did not need. Silence spread its wings, expanded my soul. My anxious thoughts were somehow dissipated, mixed with hope and expectation by the combination of words and action. Kneeling recalled everything that the clay had taught me about being present, actively engaged, ready to hear The Encourager saying, "Be here now."

I was not aware of the deep cellular level of trust that was developing inside of me until I went home to Bellingham, Washington, to be with my parents that Christmas. In the Calvinist church of my childhood, no one kneeled! And Communion was not offered regularly, so I missed two Sundays of my weekly ritual, as well as my daily practice of kneading clay.

By the time I returned to New Hampshire, where I was living then, my body was tight and tense, my thoughts were treading the endless squirrel cage inside my mind, and I could hardly breathe. But on my first day back at work, when I knelt on the floor of my studio to knead the clay, I could begin to feel my anxious thoughts drop down into my body, deeper with every breath, and finally come together where hand and clay engaged in the spiral of kneading. I knew then that kneading and kneeling had become a spiritual practice for life!

Now, nearly three decades since I began potting, I know that kneading can happen in many different ways, but all begin with routine, repeated body motions. What we normally discount as tasks to be done before the real work begins can be the basis for prayer practice in daily life. Simple actions like brushing teeth, shaving, taking a shower, doing dishes, or dressing can be the starting point for gathering our scattered thoughts, images, and fragments of consciousness. With attention to breathing and silence, we can be in *this* moment, *this* space. We can drop the focus of our awareness down into our bodies . . . until words and images begin to arise from within instead of bombarding our ears from outside. This kind of body prayer then becomes accessible to all of us who live fast and frantic lives. The four stages of kneading — attending to body rhythms, belly breathing, practicing silence and inner hearing — can be a way to reconnect with God's I AM inside.

Journal Questions

1. *Focus on a time of change you didn't want. Outline the facts as you remember them.*
2. *Then notice the larger forces working on you then and color those in your journal, using broad bands of color.*
3. *Name or describe what "fed your soul" at that time.*

GROUP: *Pair up and share whatever parts of your journal reflections you choose with your partner. Then, standing in a circle, nonverbally express your passage through a time of change.*

Kneading as Communion

"THIS is my body . . ." Jesus said as he broke the bread at the Last Supper. Could he have been looking at the disciples instead of the bread as he spoke those words? *This* body of believers. *This* time was different from all the others. *This* moment required a different kind of attention, a different kind of presence and inner hearing. His words may have been referring more to the gathered company of his friends — which probably included the women serving — than to the bread itself, as he began to prepare them for the changes ahead. He breathed new life into an old Passover ritual when he called their attention to what he was doing: "This body," here and now. In that upper room Jesus stood at the boundary between physical and metaphysical reality, as Miriam and Elizabeth had before him, with a sense of readiness for whatever would come.

Just as Jesus invited his closest friends around that table to prepare for his experience of passing through death to new life, so we, too, need to gather the disparate parts of our lives together in preparation for change. No final decisions have to be made, but we must collect the parts of our selves into one place and begin working with the whole piece or problem, even if that inner work is basically unconscious. Old patterns surface. New needs pull and stretch traditions into a workable mixture for change.

As we gather ourselves in our internal "upper room" — the place of the soul where love and aliveness dwell — we can breathe deeply and naturally from the holy center of our lives. We can begin to let ourselves know that the past can be reshaped. Breathing makes a place where we can be collected and engaged in the present moment, not simply waiting for something in the future.

When we choose silence, we create inner space for reflection and wonder. Then we can gather input for change from less obvious sources under the surface of things, like mystics who can discern the subtle signs of inner and outer harmony in a world where noise and chaos seem to rule. When we turn our ears toward the still, small voice of inner guidance, attention to the spiritual source of life comes. When we come to that kneading place of body prayer, we put ourselves in a place of readiness for whatever form is coming.

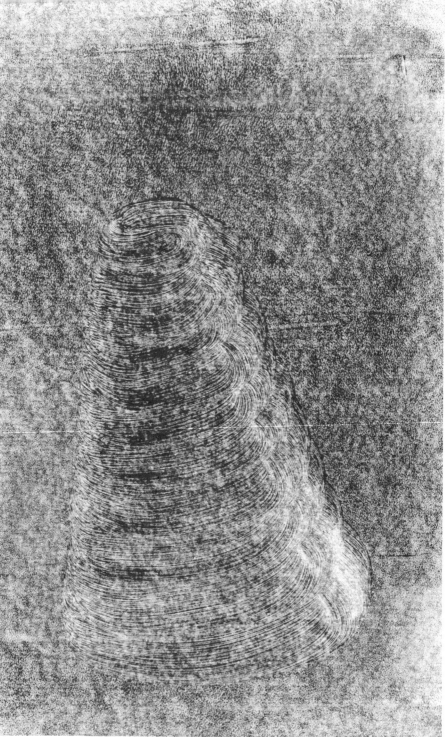

Chapter 3

CENTERING

BRINGING THE POSSIBILITIES INTO FOCUS

*Centering is a dance of opposing forces
that brings a pot into the first stage of being.
The spinning wheel throws the clay outward,
and the potter's hands press inward,
drawing all parts toward the still point
at the middle of the wheel.
The dialogue between hand and clay begins.
Nothing is cut out or left protruding from the whole;
all is mixed in by pressure from the potter's hands.
As the mound shifts to find the path of least resistance,
friction between hand and clay lessens.
As the wheel turns every part past well-braced hands,
the spinning mound becomes smooth, slick and solid.
Centering is complete
when the spinning motion is not visible to the eye,
and the surface feels smooth and balanced.*

ONCE MY POTTER'S WHEEL begins to turn, I must reckon with another variable besides the speed of the wheel: the momentum created by spinning the mass of clay under my hands. It has its own mass and direction, which is increased by the spinning wheel. Its substance and character emerge as the clay loses its undefined lumpiness and becomes a glistening cone in the center of the wheel. Speed makes the "otherness" of a particular piece of clay more obvious, and I must contend directly with its nature and potential. Centering is like conception: From a state of no being or character, suddenly the clay *is*!

The otherness of the clay engages my whole attention because I must pull the clay toward center. It wants to separate, fly off in little pieces with the wheel's speed. I use the strength of my whole body to draw all parts of the clay inward, toward the center of the wheel, until the clay appears to stand still, balanced and ready. In centering, I set my will and energy toward integration, against the forces of separation. From the blissful state of repetitive motion that kneading can produce, centering moves me into focus on the nature and being of this particular piece of clay, on all that is between the clay and me in the here and now.

TOUCH

Centering begins with touch, with direct physical contact. Distance will not do the job. No amount of thinking will move the clay — it must be held, forced, guided, and drawn toward even distribution at the center of the spinning wheel. My hands move toward the middle from opposite sides of the clay mound, pressing hard as the clay spins. We are engaged, the clay and I. My arms and shoulders tighten with effort as friction between us actually slows the wheel. I become aware of our differences, and I notice how foreign the clay feels. My will and intention stiffen as I take the measure of the clay. We are committed to this engagement now.

Physical touch also brings me into the present, engages me with a sense of living presence between us. Something new is being born. Direct contact rescues my soul from diffusion and escape, calling me to confront the challenge of dealing with "the other," what is not me or mine. Difficulty demands my attention, and clay that is still stiff and angular requires muscle to move it. If I try to smooth the friction by wetting my hands with water, I will soften the clay — something I may regret later. So I make choices about the amount of pressure to bring, the force of my being in this relationship. I must extend myself beyond convenience or comfort for the sake of something greater. Touch engages my body-self in the act of gathering in all parts, setting my effort against their tendency to fly off the wheel and scatter about the room.

Focus

As I feel the clay's protrusions lessen under my hands, I am drawn into the present moment, smoothing diversions of body and mind as I begin to focus on this piece of clay and no other. The clay has no shape yet, but it has mass and bulk. It has a sense of being, aliveness and reality. It *is*, as though conceived by the meeting of hand and the wheel's momentum. From the many possibilities touched in the kneading process, centering requires focus on just one, this one. Past and future condense into the present moment. The centered clay is poised and ready for a creating dialogue.

In the same way that the potter focuses during centering, when we make choices in a field with many potentials, we need to focus on each choice. What the wheel would fling away is contained and drawn back until the whole mass is thoroughly mixed and stabilized. What our minds would rather ignore must be considered, softened, and integrated. All diversions coalesce into a single possibility. From diffused awareness, centering moves us to focused consciousness as opposing forces find their balance point.

DIALOGUE

The word "centering" is commonly associated with breathing and body-awareness by those who meditate. The traditional meditation posture that comes to mind is of someone sitting cross-legged, eyes closed and mind alert but empty of images, breathing slowly. People who struggle with stressful jobs are taught to center in this way in order to dissociate from the desires and demands of their work.

For the potter, however, centering means dialogue between hand and clay, a visceral connection between two distinct entities. Instead of detachment, a certain kind of attachment or relatedness begins. When I am centering clay, I know that I am in a heated dialogue with that particular piece of clay. Back and forth we speak by pushing and resisting pressure. Sometimes it takes several minutes to cone the clay upward and cup it down again, using the centrifugal force of the clay to fold it inward. Such dialogue requires respect for the other, acknowledgment of limits as well as possibilities, and, finally, a mutual agreement about direction.

True dialogue honors the identity of both parties. One does not ignore the other. Instead, their dialogue is a principle of cooperation toward a single goal, of mutual commitment. If I am fighting the clay or forcing it toward a shape that its nature cannot sustain, the rest of the process will not go well. Although my spirit may idealize what I want the clay to do, my soul engages in conversation with the clay, which has substance, density, and mutual toughness. Clay is surprisingly hard to move. When the proper exchange has not taken place, the soul knows — even when spirit might justify another choice as right or good or smart.

FIELD

As I enter a relationship with a particular piece of clay, I gather the future into the present. What *is* includes what can be. I become aware of the general field of possibilities in which our conversation is taking place. Fully engaged at thought and feeling levels, I see beyond the lump of clay in front of me to what it might become. My dreams have an anchor point in the present. I consider how this mound of clay fits with what I have already created for a kiln-load and what is needed next week in my shop. I see the clay in a larger context.

Centering creates a kind of kairos moment — a moment of "is-ness" — when the past and future stand in balance with each other in a larger landscape of possibilities, relating to the present in tangible form. Finding the right balance between these opposing forces is a principle of centering. Yet it is not a balance we come to through thought and problem-solving; we find this point intuitively, beyond our reason and will. Centering is a dance of masculine and feminine, of logos and eros, of logic and love, leaning first one way and then another.

Centering can draw in the shadow or hidden parts of our past experience, so tragedy and abuse can become part of the dialogue with possibilities, opening the way for healthier balance. The future is open. And when we know that the future holds many possibilities instead of a single form, we can choose hope instead of fear. We can stand in a complex field of options without being overwhelmed. We can use the focus and attentiveness of centering to act from our physical and spiritual core, instead of meeting someone else's expectations. Like the clay standing centered on the wheel, we can be unique and still be in relation to others, continuing the dialogue, the dance of opposing forces.

Journal Questions

1. *Choose a small object that you feel attracted to. Spend a few minutes with your eyes closed, touching the surface, drawing it toward the center of your mind.*
2. *Put the object down and close your eyes again, keeping the object in focus.*
3. *With your eyes still closed, draw the object with one continuous line without lifting your pencil from the paper.*
4. *Now look at your drawing with soft eyes and an open heart, letting yourself take in the spirit expressed by your drawing.*

GROUP: Tell a story of this object, letting yourself feel a connection to this object.

CENTERING STORIES: BIBLICAL WOMEN

We are told of two women, two outcasts, who encountered the "divine otherness" in a centering dialogue. Hagar in the Hebrew Scriptures and the Samaritan Woman at the Well in the New Testament are both seen and heard by God, questioned about their identity. In response, both returned to an adverse situation with their lives changed from the inside out.

Hagar met EL ROI — the God who sees — in the desert as she faced sure death. Their dialogue was enough to empower her to return for almost fifteen years until her son grew up and they left Abraham's household the second time, for good. The Samaritan Woman moved from the margin to the center of her village through her encounter with Jesus, who, she relates, "told me all about my life," although the story indicates that Jesus mostly listened and received her truth. For both women, their many parts were brought into sharp focus by their singular encounter with God.

HAGAR'S STORY
(Genesis 16; 25:12-18)

I was invisible to them
as they argued about God's promise
and hoped for a child.
She got older and angrier,
and he clung to his prayers, as though that would help.

Doesn't he know
a woman must be younger than Sarah?
Doesn't he know I could bear them a child?

Finally, *she* noticed my body,
decided I should go in to his tent,
to lie with Abraham.

It didn't take long for us to conceive,
but during the time we were trying,
everything changed between Sarah and me.

Abraham changed, too:
He grew young again as he dreamed of a son.
My body responded, grew ripe with his love,
while Sarah aged even more, jealous and angry,
though it had been *her* plan.

She would be thoughtful one minute
and raving the next,
like steam exploding a rock.
She complained that I looked on her with contempt.
That wasn't true;

I just felt sorry for her.
What could I do?

She became more harsh and unpredictable.
I never knew what to expect . . .
a slap or a morsel of food "for the baby."

Finally, I had no choice
but to run away and hide in the desert!
I ran to a spring that I knew of
where I could wait for a caravan or herder
who might take me far from Sarah's anger.

Night fell.
Animals began to come for water.
I could hear them fighting for space,
snarling and splashing
as I crouched by a thorn bush,
terrified.

God help me!
Send someone soon.
Please, please protect me — for the child's sake.

"Hagar, slave of Sarah . . ."

Who's that?
Have I been seen? Discovered?
Where are you?
Why can't I see you?

Nothing moved.
No one spoke.
But the night was alive with a presence.
Warm. Close.
I knew someone was watching me.

Who are you? (Oh God, save me.)
Show yourself. (Oh God, give me courage.)

"Where are you going?"

What? Who are you?
You ask where I'm going?
I don't know.
Wherever I can.
I want to get away, far, far away.

"Go back," the voice replied,
"for the sake of the child, go back.
Don't be afraid. You shall live.
You will have many descendants.
And because you cried out to God,
you shall name him Ishmael, 'God hears.' "

Then I knew it was God.

The God of no name and no image
saw me in the darkness;
called me by name
and gave me a promise
that would take time to unfold.

So I went back.
Somehow I trusted this One
who came to me in the desert.
This God of Abraham and Sarah became my God, too,
and the child in my womb
became a sign of God's promise to me.
Their mysterious God of no name
saw me in the hour of my need
and came when I cried out.
So I called this God EL ROI, "the God who sees."

I turned my face back toward the tents of Abraham,
trusting EL ROI to protect me and the child from Sarah,
but I did not tell them of my promise from God.

Even though Sarah claimed my son as her own,
I knew Ishmael was the child of my body:
bone of my bone and flesh of my flesh.
I will always be his mother,
and his children will carry my spirit forward in time
for many generations.
Knowing EL ROI was with me gave me new strength
to stand in Sarah's gaze and not be afraid.

I stopped looking to Abraham to save me.
I began to see and hear for myself.

As the years passed,
my relationship with EL ROI deepened
to a presence that is with me always,
even now, as I make my way back to Egypt
with my son.

Journal Questions

1. *Negative, as well as positive, influences can bring about change. When have you been "squeezed" by a difficult or uncomfortable relationship?*
2. *Have you ever reached a "breaking point" and fled or withdrawn into depression? What was that time like for you?*
3. *When have you felt "heard" and "seen" so that it made a difference in your life?*

GROUP: As an exercise in being seen and heard, pair up and stand back to back without touching. Then slowly let your backs touch; then let your hands touch on one side; turn and make eye contact. Say a quiet, "Hello, _____," using your partner's name. When you are ready, discuss with your partner how you felt seen and recognized. Then talk as a group about being seen and heard this way.

THE SAMARITAN WOMAN'S STORY
(John 4:1-42)

There are many ways to be touched by another person.
I know the physical ways all too well.
After years of excuses and abuses,
I ran away from the last of five brothers
who passed me from one to the next,
trying to fulfill their duty to sire an heir for the eldest
who died soon after we married.

Yes, I live with the shame of having no child,
but it makes my life at the edge of society easier.
We each have our ways to survive.
My way is a man who is not my husband,
but he is good to me, so I stay.

I go at noon to the well claimed by our forefather, Jacob,
to avoid gossip and taunting from the other women.
There I have time to think about other things.
Try to make sense of my life —
think about what's right and wrong for me —
wrestle with my choices, as Jacob did.

I think of his wives, Rachel and Leah,
and wonder if they watched for a sign
of God's presence as I do.
Especially Leah, the older one whom Jacob did not love.
Sometimes I feel close to Leah, the elder sister:
Not cherished. Not his beloved.
An outcast in her own home.

We Samaritans have been cast out by the Jews,
rejected as unclean because we intermarried,
but I know we all come from Jacob's stock.
"One source, one savior,"
I say to myself when I pray.
I feel only a little guilty when I do that.

As I said, there are many ways to be touched by someone.

I saw him first by the well
when I came alone at mid-day.
I approached anyway
because it was too hot to go back,
and he didn't seem threatening.
I was sweating with my heavy jar, glad to set it down.
He cleared his throat and asked me for a drink,
as though his throat was dry.
Maybe he was as nervous as I was,

alone by the well.
He might as well have touched me with lightning!

What?
You, a Jew,
ask me, a Samaritan,
for a drink?

He smiled and nodded,
so I gave him my ladle.
He simply ignored the rules
and drank naturally from the bucket,
as though he were in his own home!
He gave thanks to God for the water and for me.
I was stunned for a moment.
(You'll probably think I was crazy for doing this,
but I brushed his hand,
to make sure he was real.)

Then, as though he had heard my deepest questions,
the very thirsting of my soul,
he made a strange remark:
"If you knew who was asking,
you would have asked him for *living* water!"

Well, I'm not stupid!
I didn't hesitate to ask for the living water!
Then he switched the subject and asked for my husband.
A-ha! I thought.
He's not so free of the rules as he appears.

He acted as though the question of my husband
was more to reassure himself

that *I* knew who I was
than to get information he did not have.
I never met anyone, man or woman,
who responded to my story that way.
He simply said it was true.
Nothing else. No law. No judgment.
I decided he must be a prophet,
able to see with God's eyes,
knowing the truth that I'd run from.

My questions seemed to touch him,
invite him to go further.
Our dialogue danced back and forth,
each of us speaking from the heart,
moving deeper and deeper
into kinship that captured something
I always felt here by the well of our common ancestor.

I felt centered and whole,
drawn in by his words,
clearly separate and yet deeply connected.
Focused and still,
as though the I AM of God was between us.

He must be a prophet.
And not just a prophet,
but the one we — even Samaritans —
were waiting for from the house of Israel,
Then he said it, quietly, to me alone: "I am he."

Just then I noticed his disciples coming back from the village.
I could see them gesturing and talking, pointing at me.
I must confess that I felt afraid I would lose myself again,

so I ran.
I set down my jar,
as though it were full of all the things
I wanted to leave behind,
and ran back to the village,
freed of the shame and guilt
that had kept me apart from my people.
I called out to everyone,
"Come and see the man
who told me everything I ever did!"

Something in me must have seemed different to them, too.
The townspeople gathered and followed me back to the well.
The stranger's followers crowded around him as we came,
trying to protect him, I guess.

But we weren't going to attack.
Far from it.
Even the village elders joined us, crowding around me,
asking questions, breaking old taboos with every step!
It must have been a sight for God to see,
watching us meet there in the desert
around the well that Jacob named.

This stranger told us that the realm of God was here,
now, in our hearts.
We could still go to worship in the high places, he said,
but we did not need to.
No longer did we have to seek out a priest to approach God.
Each of us could have the well of living water inside.

What I felt on that first day, by the well, has continued.
Though others have come to their own beliefs,

I know inside that I have been set free of the past,
free to love without giving my body away as worthless.
Jesus (for that was his name)
let me know that I touched him deeply
with my honesty and my questions —
fed his weary soul in a way
that his disciples had not been able to.
He even called me an evangelist!
I was only doing what seemed natural:
sharing the living water that I found inside.

Journal Questions

1. Recall and write down a chance encounter that changed your life in some way.
2. Where in this encounter did you experience a sense of "the holy"?
3. The woman's water jar was a symbol of her daily tasks. What is the symbol of yours?

GROUP: Share words or symbols of your daily work and create a centering space to set them down for a time of talking together.

CENTERING DIALOGUE

Not only did the act of centering clay teach me about touching and gathering in the hard and soft parts of my life, but it also changed my openness to touch. I began to let other people touch me, physically and figuratively. Repeating the centering rhythms over and over again drew the scattered parts of my life together until I could focus my sense of self in my body and reach out to others without fear of disappearing or being absorbed. Centering in my body made it possible for me to make new choices about what to do, what to say, how to be with another person in a larger field of people, things, ideas, and impulses.

About two years after I started potting, I went to visit my grandmother for the last time. In earlier years she had been a vital, active woman, both seamstress and carpenter, capable of shingling a roof and grafting fruit trees. But now she lay speechless in bed at the Dutch nursing home, waiting to die. I could not imagine anything I might do to ease her journey. Because she had suffered a massive stroke, we could not even be sure she recognized anyone. I had avoided the visit because I did not know what to say.

Finally, I felt centered enough to go. She appeared to be dozing as I entered her room, so I stood at the foot of her bed, drinking in the silence and the scene, breathing deeply — as I often did during preparation times in my studio.

My body knew what to do, even if my brain did not. I remembered a small bottle of hand lotion I kept in my purse for softening my hands after a session with clay. I pulled back the sheet and saw her dry, curled feet, much smaller than I remembered. I took out the lotion, warmed it by rubbing my hands together, and began to stroke her feet. Her eyes fluttered but stayed closed. I simply continued, letting my hands get the feel of her bones and calluses. My focus grew as I felt her skin soften and saw it turn pinker with new circulation.

Feelings of love flooded me, spreading through my hands and feet, my body, until the whole room seemed alive. When I looked up with soft eyes, she was looking at me with the same presence I felt inside. Not blank or lost, as she had

been on other occasions, she was fully present and connected at the heart level.

I saw a tear slide out of the corner of her eye and realized
my cheeks were wet, too. We stood together at the edge of
that mysterious boundary between life and death — ready
and yet wordless. Time stood still. Tenderness spoke beyond
words, and I felt released from the guilt that had kept me
away. "Good-bye, Grandma," I whispered. "I love you."

All the parts of my self were gathered into her room in
that kairos moment. We saw and heard each other in true
communion. She was the first to take me close to the border
between living and dying. We touched each other in a
dialogue that continues to this day, beyond the death of her
body and the aging of mine: She still appears in my dreams.
For the first time, the centering that had taken place inside
my body in the pottery studio had become visible on the
outside.

Journal Questions

1. *Reflect on a time spent with someone who was gravely
   ill or dying. Describe any moments of deep communion
   that you shared.*
2. *Now shift your focus to the separateness that you felt
   during this communion time — the otherness of that
   person and your own aliveness.*
3. *Using crayons in your non-dominant hand, color a picture
   of this communion time.*

GROUP: *Place your color forms together on a centering cloth,
holding these sacred encounters in silence as a community.
Leave time for sharing the stories, if it seems appropriate.*

CENTERING AS COMMUNION

When we center ourselves, we find an internal sense of direction for change. Other possibilities are set aside, and we focus on the one before us, going deeper as the soul engages, draws inward, and finds the living core. "This *IS* my body," Jesus said to his friends, focusing their attention on the aliveness of the moment — the "is-ness" — of what they could see and feel and taste and hear right then.

In the midst of their fear, Jesus drew the disciples toward a new state of being, a new center. "My body is here, is now, in you," he was saying. All the other moments of his touch and presence were suddenly present in his simple gesture of breaking bread. He was showing them how to draw from the well, the "living water" of his spirit, the soul of their community, once he was gone. The disciples were included in a new way by Jesus' words and action at the Last Supper.

His gesture and his words made tangible the change they dreaded most. As the outside pressures increased and talk of death made them conscious that Jesus would soon be gone, unhealed spots in their fellowship began to surface: "Who gets to sit on his right hand?" argued James and John. "You'll never wash my feet," said Peter. "One of you will betray me," said Jesus. Each crass and very human response to Jesus was revealed that night as they were drawn close, as much by their questions and his changes in the Passover celebration as by the pressures from outside. Their common soul was being gathered as their differences, human anger and jealousy, were included. They were being centered, not perfected!

Like Hagar when she was seen and heard by God in the desert, the disciples were being drawn into a new state of being by the force of Jesus' hands and words. As they tried to hang onto old ways, old needs, and old patterns, the power of Jesus' vision pulled them toward a new sense of purpose. As the disciples tried to fling themselves away from what this Communion symbolized, Jesus firmly drew them back to the reality of the present: "This *is* my body . . ."

The awe-full intensity of Jesus' words and the disciples' response was deepened by the surrounding silence of those who served the Passover meal — presumably the women around Jesus — for all knew that this night was different from all other nights, different from all other Passover celebrations. This time, the angel of death would not pass by their household. But Jesus was not resigned or despairing. Instead, out of the terror and anguish, something new was being brought into focus. Every act, every move was brought into terrible clarity as the disciples struggled to understand what Jesus was saying and doing.

Like the Samaritan Woman, the disciples were touched and drawn to the center, to the "living water" in themselves. As their focus deepened, their dialogue revealed both pain and fear of change. Perhaps only Jesus saw the larger field of time and space in which this particular act of Communion was taking place. He knew the center would have to be recreated, not preserved. His death would take away one form of God's I AM and call forth another kind of soul in this frightened body of believers.

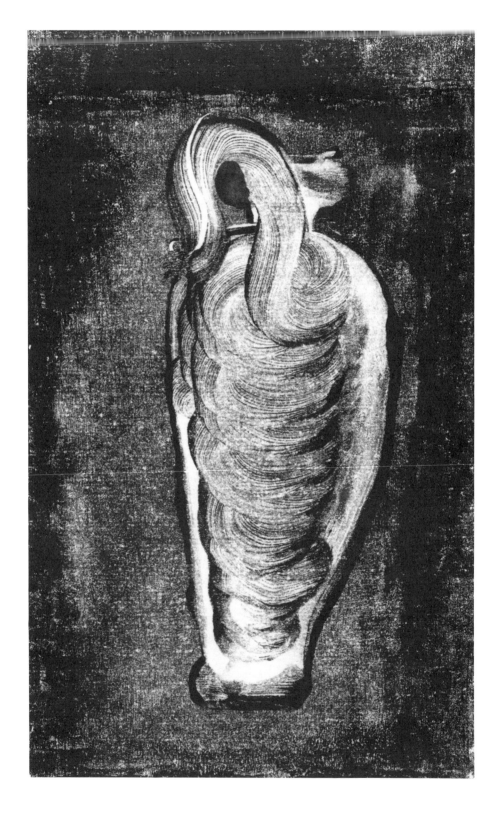

Chapter 4

SHAPING

MAKING CHOICES

After centering the clay,
a potter opens the solid mound by making a hole in the middle.
Then one hand can work from the inside
and the other from outside,
squeezing the clay between them at a single point of tension
where all the change is concentrated.
Using her body to steady and brace her hands,
the potter "throws" the clay by pressing firmly and evenly
in an upward spiral to thin the wall
and stretch the clay to its full height.
After the initial "pull" into a straight-sided pot,
the potter can then change the shape
by pressing harder with one hand or the other,
to swell or constrict the form.
Excess clay is trimmed from the bottom,
and the lip or top rim is thickened slightly
to hold the shape and please the eye.

THROWING A POT is an exercise of counter-vailing pressures, intentionality, and congruence between the inner and outer surfaces. As my inner hand begins to define the space inside, I am aware of a "spirit force" inside of me, longing for shape and form in the world. As my outer or centering hand supports the thinning clay wall, I am aware of the need for structure, commitment, and routine. What begins as an emerging concept takes on shape and substance as finger-pressure translates my intention into the clay, as I make intuitive choices every instant. Attending to inner and outer pressures makes adjustments possible and choices necessary — both in working clay and in living life. Inner and outer pressures combine to shape my soul, stretching me beyond the predictable balance of a straight-sided cylinder toward my unique shape and purpose.

PRESSURE

Opening a hole in the middle of a centered mound of clay is easy. I lean into the clay with my upper body weight, testing the strength of the clay against mine in a slow push. My thumbs press downward through the clay toward the center of the wheel. Then, filling the well I have created with water to keep the clay movable, I use my inside hand to pull a thick ring of clay outward where it will be used to make the entire wall of the pot. The centrifugal force of the spinning wheel helps this expanding movement, moving the clay toward the edge of the wheel. What I think of as the "spirit space" of the pot expands naturally with the wheel, swelling outward like an infant taking its first full breath. The pot seems alive as the inner cavity grows.

At the same time, my outside hand applies strong counterpressure, cupping and holding the clay to keep the spinning mass from flinging itself off the wheel. Sometimes, if I have put too much water on the surface in an attempt to keep the clay sliding smoothly between the friction of my opposing fingers, a fine slurry of clay sprays everything in its path.

Moist and smooth and moving, the clay feels like muscle. We resist each other, body to body, as I move the clay into a fat ring on the wheelhead. I am conscious of my opposing hands, one creating space and the other containing the motion, bracing the outer surface to set the limit of expansion. They need each other, these two hands. They are the opposing forces in me made visible — creative eros, flinging my spirit outward from the core, and conserving logos, keeping impulse from destruction. Loving and limiting, in step with the music of motion.

I take a deep breath, as though preparing to dive into a pool, and then I begin to pull the clay upward in a long, slow spiral of pressure, one hand against the other, through the clay. I concentrate on the single point of tension where my fingers on either side of the wall are nearly touching through the clay. That is where change happens — where the tension is greatest.

With each pull, the cylinder wall grows thinner and more vulnerable. Lumps of thickness or an air bubble jump to the surface between my fingers, and without thinking I lessen the pressure on thin spots to keep the wall from tearing. Close attention creates a kind of intimacy with the pot as I explore the clay's thinness and elasticity. I am surprised to find that I am holding my breath a little, as though waiting to see what possibilities the clay has hidden from my earlier touch. At the same time, I learn to trust the clay's capacity for extension and change. With intimacy and trust comes love, even for a clay vessel.

INTENTION

With my fingers still working together on opposite sides of the clay, I then unbalance my touch and let one hand or the other predominate to express my artistic intention for this pot. More pressure from my inner hand will flare the pot outward with the wheel's motion. Pressure from my outer hand will curve the wall inward, thickening the wall and constricting the shape at the belly, shoulder, or neck. The shape emerges quickly with each pull.

As the wall gets thinner, my options narrow because certain moves cannot be reversed without collapsing the entire form. Each decision, each direction, makes a difference. As my hands keep the clay in tension, the body of the clay takes on an individual shape. My vision of the finished pot is especially important as I complete this basic action of throwing or shaping, even though the pot is far from finished. While there is still room for change, my intention comes strongly into play, giving the pot identity and purpose.

CONGRUENCE

Finally, the visible outside shape and the invisible inner surface come to match each other. Although I watch the outline of the pot in a mirror that sits directly in front of my wheel, I also "watch" with my fingers deep inside the cavity that has grown inside the pot. I feel for harmony between the outer shape and the inner space, between appearance and soul. If a pot is thick in some places and thin in others, uneven shrinkage during drying or firing may cause cracks to develop. Then the pot's potential is quite different from what it would have been as an evenly thick pot. When I am throwing well, congruence is not a question I have to struggle with. It simply happens. The clay seems to sing and settle into its own shape.

When the basic shape is completed, I work especially with the lip, or top rim, to make sure it is smooth and appropriate to the rest of the form. My sense of wholeness is reflected in the shapes I make. For me, a thick lip can ruin a good cup; a thin lip can weaken a strong bowl. Thickening a curl of clay around the top rim has a practical function, as well as an aesthetic one, because the lip holds the form "into round" when I later cut the soft clay from the wheelhead and lift it to a drying rack.

As I come to the end of the shaping process, specific details become more important: Should the neck be more defined? The shoulder lifted? Belly rounded? From the general category of "a pot," I concentrate on making it "my" pot, my work, my vision. I have to trust my sense of the whole piece to tell me when the shaping is done, when a pot is congruent inside and out, lip and body. In the same way, I look for a match between soul and action in my life. Attention to both internal and external reality is necessary if we are to withstand the difficulties we can predict, knowing full well there will be others we cannot imagine. Shaping our lives takes a parallel level of concentration that is as attentive to the invisible matters of spirit as to the outer world of conflicts and commitments.

Journal Questions

1. *Make a line drawing of your body in your journal.*
2. *Use color to identify external pressures you feel.*
3. *Use another color to identify any internal pressures you feel. Reflect on your drawing. What does this drawing reveal?*

GROUP: Identify one pair of pressures that seem to be squeezing you at a point of change. Share your insights.

Shaping Stories: Biblical Women

Two successful extroverts in the Bible discovered their inner strengths, as pressure from the outside met surprising inward knowing to reveal their true identities. The first woman, a Judge from Tekoa, used her wit and sense of timing to remind King David that only the living can make new choices. Her gentle pressure allowed him to act out of a deeper source of love than out of the revenge he had decreed for his favorite son, Absalom. The second woman, Martha of Bethany, was not afraid to pressure Jesus with her anger at his lateness when her brother, Lazarus, died. She was not afraid to object to the smell when Jesus ordered the tomb opened. And she was free to celebrate their own "last supper": She had learned to listen to her inner wisdom through these events.

The Judge from Tekoa
(II Samuel 14:1-24)

Ach! Families are all the same!

Violence. Abuse. What will become of us?
Everyone in Jerusalem knows the story . . .
Absalom killed his own brother,
who had raped their sister, Tamar.
Then Absalom's father, King David,
banished the young warrior forever . . .
but now the King misses Absalom so much
he can't make decisions about other matters.
That much is common gossip.

When a messenger arrived in Tekoa, asking for me,
I could not imagine what was about to unfold.
He asked me to come with him to Jerusalem
and meet with Joab, the King's commander.

How could I resist!
As a small-town judge, and a woman at that,
being asked to meet with the most powerful man
next to David was very flattering.
So, I agreed to come.

I knew Joab's job was to keep peace in the kingdom,
but he could hardly do that
if the king's own household was tearing itself apart!

Knowing that Absalom might be gathering
a rebel force against the King,
Joab must have been desperate
to get the King to change his mind
and let Absalom return.
Asking me to come was a sign of Joab's concern,
though not for me, I'm sure.

He had known of my work for many years.
Flattered me by calling me a wise woman on occasion.
We'd both have a chance to see
how wise I could be under pressure!

I've had lots of experience helping people
find a way out of their own stubborn threats.
Tekoa may be a small town,

but I've dealt with all kinds of people, rich and poor.
Down deep, they're all the same —
a mixture of love and hate.
I like to think I've been important
in shaping the town where I live.

I care about families,
and I care about the King,
though he's hardly more than a bandit in my estimation.
Still, I sense that God is with him.
His rule hasn't brought peace in Tekoa,
but I am hopeful that it will.

We need a code of laws that will stop these family feuds.
The men get maimed or killed,
and the women get caught in between, like Tamar did.
As a father, the King pined for both the living and the dead.
As a King, he was bound by his own edict.
I hoped the father would prevail.
So, I went to Jerusalem to meet with Joab.

We decided I would present a case like David's
and ask the King to stop the feud.
Then, when the time was right,
I would confront the King with his own mercy!
Get him to change his edict,
let Absalom come home.

The first part was easy.
I told a story about my own son
who had killed someone in a family feud.
I described how our line
was being threatened with extinction

because the victim's family was out for vengeance:
an eye for an eye, a life for a life.
King David understood immediately
how destructive that would be.
He offered his protection
so my son could come home without fear for his life.
That's how the more obvious part of the problem was solved.

Then I pushed the King to invoke the Lord God
as an even greater source of assurance for me.
So David gave me God's protection as well.

I thought — rightly, as it turned out —
that if we both stood as human beings
under the mercy of God,
David also would be able to see himself
as the subject of God's mercy.
Then it would be harder for him
to stay with his own angry judgment.

After I finished my story,
and David had given me God's protection
as well as his royal pledge,
I asked to speak to him directly,
as one person to another.
In my experience as a judge,
I've found it useful to step beyond the legal balancing
of one side against the other
and talk directly to the plaintiffs . . .
but I've also learned to be careful about the timing.

When he said I could speak candidly,
I reminded him that the Lord God does not take away life

to avenge a death.
"Death is like water spilled on the ground," I said,
"it can never be recovered."
"I know," he said. "One son is dead
and another might as well be."
"Only the living can make other choices," I said,
"so let us live together."

I then went on to speak of Absalom.
Fury came and went on David's face
as I spoke, hardly stopping to breathe.
But he listened,
much to my surprise and to his credit.
I could see his face begin to soften
as the father in him began to win out over the King.
Finally, he spoke.
Said the boy could come home safely,
though he still refused to see Absalom.

As I turned to leave,
congratulating myself for standing firm before the King,
he stopped me with a question:
"Did Joab put you up to this?"

I might have lied,
but I remembered that I, too,
had stood on common ground before our God,
so I confessed the truth.

I waited for the King's anger to blaze against Joab or me,
but somehow he had touched the source of love
and let his heart embrace us both.

I watched the father in him win and reach for change,
although I knew he planned to keep some part of his hate
and would not speak to Absalom when he returned.

Once the audience was over,
I traveled back to Tekoa,
as just another small-town judge.
Anonymous really,
but deeply satisfied that my skills had a greater purpose
in bringing God's intentions into human shape.

Journal Questions

1. *What external pressures do you associate with your work (paid or not)?*
2. *When have you taken risks because of your beliefs or values in your workplace (home, office, church, etc.)?*
3. *What were your hopes or intentions in taking one such risk?*

GROUP: Do you feel satisfied with the match between your inner capacities and your outer activities? If not, what would you like to change? Talk together about any changes you would like to make in your working situation.

MARTHA'S STORY
(Luke 10:38-42; John 11; 12:1-10)

For the past three years,
our house has been a place to be,
to rest, to talk and pray
for Jesus and his disciples
as they come to Bethany

on their way to Jerusalem.
Mary and I have our different ways
of being with Jesus:
Her way is more inward,
prayerful and quiet;
mine is more outward,
practical and public.
I like to think Jesus is drawn to both:
my way of caring for him, and hers.

Lazarus and Mary
like to sit with Jesus
when he comes.
I would, too, if I had the time,
but there is much to do.
The house is always ready,
but meals require extra shopping and preparation,
cspccially when the others accompany him.

He's teaching them,
preparing them to be a family
of choice, not blood.
I try to understand
but know my place is to contain and hold.

My favorite times are when he comes alone.
He's like the older brother I don't have.
He chides me a bit for being bossy,
but then we laugh.
Oh, I do love having him here.
That's why it was so hard for me to understand

why he didn't come right away
when I sent word when Lazarus got so sick.

I knew it was dangerous for Jesus
because we were close to Jerusalem:
The authorities were watching for him.
Feeling threatened by his popularity, I guess.
It's our own people, Pilot and his circle.
So nervous about rebellion.

I must admit, sometimes I would like to take up arms
if I thought Jesus would stand for it.
Make him the King.
What a kingdom it would be!

But, no, the Lord is more of a teacher than a ruler,
always talking about a different kind of a kingdom.
One where everyone will be welcome.

Ah, but I've given the story away.

At the time it wasn't so simple.
Lazarus got sicker and sicker.
Jesus didn't come.
I was beside myself. Furious with him.
He could have healed Lazarus,
even from a distance, I was sure!

When Jesus did come, I couldn't help myself.
I ran out and yelled at him in front of everybody!
"If you had been here, my brother would not have died!"

Then, you know what he did?
He told me Lazarus would rise again.

"I believe you," I said.
But then Jesus moved the time of rising
from a future point into the present:
"I am the resurrection now," he said.

Suddenly I felt the breath of God on my face —
the presence of God in his touch.
I could not speak.
And then I saw what he had been saying.
"Are you the one we've been waiting for?" I whispered.
He nodded.

Things happened so fast after that,
I can hardly remember.
I felt like I was coming apart — ready to fly into space —
but his eyes held me.
His touch was like fire.
I knew everything would be all right,
no matter what happened.

We went to Mary, and she accused him as I had done.
Then we went to the tomb and Jesus wept.
For Lazarus? For us? For himself?
We'll never know.

When Jesus turned to the crowd and said,
"Roll away the stone," my stomach turned.
"Oh no, Lord," I cried,

"Lazarus has been in there three days.
He stinks by now!"

But Jesus paid no attention to me.
He cried in a loud voice, "Lazarus, come out!"
And I saw a flutter of white — the grave clothes.
Like a ghost he came, slowly, still bound,
but not reeking of rot.

Everyone stood transfixed.
"Unwrap him!" Jesus said to the crowd,
breaking the spell.
I could barely move, myself.

Thank God, someone did —
let Lazarus breathe and bend finally.
He was completely whole and well again!
Everyone was ecstatic
to have Lazarus back from the dead!
But there were some officials from Jerusalem
who seemed angry, even afraid of Jesus.
Maybe the local priest, too.

We didn't invite them to the banquet we had
just before Passover,
you may be sure of that!
But everyone else was welcome.
We could not have kept them away.

I sat Lazarus and Jesus at the head table,
and we had a great celebration!

It was a grand affair, if I do say so myself.
Mary even brought out our family jar of burial nard
and anointed Jesus' feet with it.
Lazarus and I were glad to be part of that,
even if Judas nearly spoiled her gift
by grumbling about giving it to the poor.

Poor Judas.
Always trying to spoil a good party.
But Jesus intervened.
"Leave her alone," he said,
"She saved this for the day of my burial."

And I knew then that Mary's intuition was right:
Jesus would die in Jerusalem.
This could be our last supper with him.
This time, I wept.

Journal Questions

1. Being "thin-skinned" or irritable may be a sign of your inner longings. Think back over this week and notice such times. Can you identify what your inner self might have been saying then?
2. Can you recall a time when something happened to you, or to someone close to you, that opened up a new understanding, which in turn opened into something more?

GROUP: Share an experience you have had with a group or community "unbinding" you. What dead parts of your life have been released by the caring of others?

DISCOVERING HIDDEN SHAPES

The principle of shaping — paying attention to both internal and external pressures — continually affects our choices in life. This became acutely obvious to me when we moved from Kansas back to Washington, D.C. in 1976. Outwardly, the task of finding my place as a potter was not difficult. In 1973, when we had left Washington, I had been teaching pottery for the Art League of Northern Virginia. While we had been away, the Art League had persuaded the city of Alexandria to open a derelict building on the Potomoc River as an art center. When we returned, I was juried into one of the cooperatives and joined more than a hundred artists in reclaiming an old building called the "Torpedo Factory" for studio space. I shared the rent with five partners and worked there once a week and every fifth weekend, throwing pots and talking with visitors. The structure of throwing pots and working at the Torpedo Factory was like an outer hand, containing and holding the outward thrust of my creative work.

But the inward pressure caused by our return to Washington was intense and full of grief. I had loved our Victorian house in Kansas and had developed a spiritual community there. When we moved back to Washington, I felt like my spirit was without a skin. My soul felt lost and alone. I felt ungrounded, uncentered, and shapeless. Although we had found a house with a basement room for my pottery studio and facilities in the back yard for a gas kiln, I could not seem to get started. I pulled inward and went to work as routinely as a potter throws a straight-sided cylinder — the most basic shape — knowing that my body would tell me when it was time to flare outward into a more unique shape again.

Every morning after Peter left for work, I wrote my dreams in a journal, opening myself to divine presence. Sometimes I simply sat, breathing deeply, in an attitude of expectant waiting, trying to give my inner pressures room to expand and shape my day's work. Then I would go to my studio and work in silence for an hour or so, knowing (by then) that my body could contain my longing for a spiritual home until my hands and feet could guide me there.

Shortly after our return, an old friend came to visit, bringing two salt-water maples to plant in the yard. He welcomed us back to Virginia and described a readiness for inward growth in the Episcopal church he was serving. My soul began to stir as I talked with Michael about some images I had begun to have while potting — images of inner change, of stretching and shaping people like I would a pot.

"Could you do a retreat for our church using clay?" he asked. Like the Tekoan woman, I wanted to be helpful and share my expertise. But like Martha, I was feeling angry that a Jesus-person hadn't come to save me from my depression over moving.

"Maybe I could do it next year," I said, "but not yet."

Michael went back to Virginia Beach, but we visited periodically, and I always felt his encouragement whenever the question of my doing a workshop came up. I sensed that some new form was trying to emerge, but that the inner and outer pressure had not yet thinned out the "clay" of me enough to name what the new shape was.

Peter and I began to explore membership at The Church of the Saviour, an innovative, ecumenical church in downtown Washington, D.C. In my search for a spiritual home, I took classes and entered a mission group. I also found a spiritual director and began working with issues of money and tithing as preparation for membership in the Seekers Community, one of the (now) ten small worshipping communities of the church. Those outward pressures helped to keep my inner search contained.

When I neared the end of the two-year process of moving toward membership, my spiritual director urged me to take a class in liturgical clowning. "You need to learn detachment," she said, "to learn how to relax and have a good time. You also need an experience of grace, of trusting the unknown, of letting something emerge instead of working so hard to make it happen." Clowning was the last thing I would have chosen as a catalyst for change.

I made a clear choice to let my inner life swell into a new shape, so for twelve weeks I took a clowning class. "Frieda" emerged from my dreams, complete with bushy red hair, a floppy suit with kid-drawings on it, and huge Army-green tennis shoes with red pompons. Frieda's costume and persona provided me with a new container to replace the form I had left in Kansas! Everything she touched took on a special lightness. I felt my soul grow visible as Frieda took on shape and substance.

As though on cue from a divine source, Michael asked Peter and me to lead "the first annual all-church retreat" for his church soon after Frieda was born. By then I was ready to take my potter's wheel and share images from the clay. When we planned the weekend, we knew we needed a special event for Saturday night to include the children, so we decided to incorporate Frieda, although, secretly, I wondered if she would have the courage to "come out" at the retreat.

Everything went well. People were responsive. By the time Saturday night came, the parents and children seemed ready for whatever we had to offer. After some singing, the children went off for their activities, and the adults moved into pairs for an exercise designed to stretch inward. Peter led the group in the application of imaginary clown make-up — whiteface and color. Intimacy and tenderness settled over the room as men and women gently stroked the illusory make-up on each other's faces. At one point Peter began to apply real greasepaint to my face, and I actually "went into" clown — although most people were concentrating so hard on what they were doing they did not notice.

After people had a chance to talk about the intimacy they had experienced, the music stopped. I stood, as Frieda the clown, listening, while the children came in quietly. No one spoke.

With mime gestures, I pretended to hear an imaginary cry and followed the sound to a spot in the room where I had hidden a long loaf of bread. I picked the bread up and held it to my breast like a baby. A little girl was watching me intently, transfixed. The bread/baby began to "shiver," and I looked at the little girl with questioning eyes. She took off her sweater and handed it to me to wrap the "baby" in. Something in the silence let us speak heart to heart. I glanced at Michael and saw the tears trickling down his face. Others were weeping, too. We stood on holy ground, softened and shaped by the child's response to need. My soul had finally found her home again — as a clown!

Journal Questions

1. Describe a new behavior or choice you are making, no matter how small it may be.

2. What results are you seeing? How does that choice impact other parts of your life?

3. Finding a "lost" part of yourself can be an important piece
    of shaping your wholeness. Can you identify part of your
    "hidden child" that you have discovered recently?

GROUP: With colored tissue paper, tape, and other decorative details (feathers, ribbons, etc.), make a hat that represents your inner self. Then tell about it.

SHAPING AS COMMUNION

Shaping depends on the inner hand, the inner force of one's
spirit that seeks to move beyond physical limits. Outer
pressures — mundane and even profane in appearance —
continue to be the centering or containing hand. The two,
working together, create the soul's shape and form.
Changes in shape and size happen where the inner and
outer pressures meet most intensely.

My own experience suggests that we focus attention on
the outer shape of our lives between the ages of twenty and
thirty, letting family and financial needs define our choices.
As we enter our thirties, the "spirit hand" begins to feel
confined or cramped, deforming and reforming the straight-
sided cylinder of cultural conformity. The inner hand
stretches and swells our profile, giving our lives a unique
shape in the world — or collapsing the form to begin the
process over again. This is where intention counts, where
choices are necessary for a flowing dance of change and
creativity. At midlife and beyond, our inner life becomes
more visible as the outside shape changes to accommodate
an inner force of spirit.

When Jesus was about thirty, he was baptized in the River Jordan to begin his public ministry. Then, as with the Judge from Tekoa and Martha of Bethany, his inner readiness met an outer need. He began to let the shape of his spirit be visible for others to see. For approximately three years, he taught and healed in a direct, physical way to express the fullness of God's intention for human life, but he rarely spoke of his own body. He referred only briefly to his humanity when he used the term "Son of Man." The congruence of inner and outer pressures did not become completely visible until the Last Supper, when he finally spoke of his own body and blood.

"This is *MY BODY* . . ." said Jesus, opening the process of change to another dimension. My body. My blood. Different from yours. My body, alive to the vulnerability of love and death. He withdrew from the group identity of the Passover meal into the solitude of his unique identity. As he claimed his own body-self, he gave the disciples a tangible, physical way to remember him as a partner and friend.

My body. My soul enfleshed. My work completed. My death time here and now. When Jesus was able to claim the fullness of his embodied being, he could choose the death that would be thrust upon him instead of seeking more time to change the shape of his life.

Earlier, just after his baptism, Jesus had defended himself with quotations from Scripture against Satan's temptations to be divine and avoid death. Now he faced that temptation again — and he made a choice to claim full-fillment. As he sat with his friends for the last time, his body and soul were fully congruent. At last, his words had become flesh.

As we make choices to let ourselves embody the soul-force that seeks shape and substance in space-time, we too face the temptation to deny or split off from our bodies. Shaping as communion means allowing congruence between our inner soul and outer bodies to develop until we, too, can claim our bodies as sacred.

Chapter 5

FINISHING

TRUSTING THE SOURCE
OF CREATIVITY

After a pot has been thrown on the wheel,
it is cut loose and set aside to stiffen
until the neck and shoulder will hold the weight of the pot.
Then it is inverted
to let the thickness at the bottom dry to leather hardness.
Finally, a foot is shaved with a metal cutting tool
to provide a rim that will help the pot stand
without rocking on a flat surface.
Liquid clay or "slip" may be brushed inside the rim
so that a potter can sign her name into the clay body,
claiming it as her own creation.

THERE IS NO OUTSIDE AUTHORITY to tell me when a pot is finished, no standard or rule except my own desire to explore the full potential of each piece of clay. I wait for a sense of completion, a certain knowing that I have done what I can, and then I stop. I have to care enough to quit, to let go of one thing for the next, to trust that more will come. To finish one thing and make room for the next means trusting my creative source enough to embrace endings as well as beginnings. Each ending is a little death, closing off the possibility of further change. The spell of my creativity is broken, my attention spreads from one focus to many alternatives for the next piece of clay, and the rush of joy that I get from completing a form begins to ebb. Finishing is an act of faith in the principle of renewal, which stands against my fear that nothing more will come.

The rhythm of start and finish, of foot and lip, is like breathing in and breathing out. Our bodies do it all the time: breathe out the past, breathe in the future. But being conscious of the transition moments when we stand poised between past and future takes courage and practice. Choosing to change means letting go of some things, no matter how important they are, to make space for the new. Finishing also means trusting that something in us — our spiritual source — is forever being creative, always wanting to give birth. Eros is always there in the background.

CARING

Footing a bowl makes both artist and onlooker conscious of the whole piece because footing brings closure to the creative impulse that gave birth to a particular pot. My mentor and friend, Louie Mideke, taught me to pay attention to the way a pot is finished: "Take care of the foot, and the lip and the body will take care of itself," he often said.

Since the lip is usually finished during the throwing process, the foot becomes the focus of attention as I complete each pot. Every potter has a characteristic way of "footing" a bowl. Some like it rough and others, smooth. Some like a plain foot that contrasts with the glaze to be applied later; others finish the foot with its own coat of "slip," a liquid clay that can be colored but does not run like glaze. The foot of a pot literally gives it something to stand on and lifts the body from a table surface, so light can get under it and shade the contour for better visual definition.

Being conscious of the foot and the lip, the upper and lower edge of each piece, keeps me from producing sloppy or soul-less pieces. Caring about the whole shape of each pot in this way brings me a feeling of completion and satisfaction, lets me trust what I have made. Once I have completed the foot, I make no further change in the body of a pot. It is ready to stand alone. Like Mideke's, my pots have a pronounced pedestal foot, which is brushed with an iron band marking the edge of the glaze coating and defining the clean, smooth, bare rim. The way I foot my bowls gives them a classic form and a clear statement that speaks to a viewer. My pots have a firm base and look like they can make their own way in the world.

CLAIMING

Once I have formed the foot and smoothed the bottom rim, I cover the area inside the rim with a layer of slip and sign my name through the thin coat of color, into the body itself. My signature acknowledges this pot as one of mine. Like the ancient artists in the neolithic caves of Europe and Africa who signed their work with handprints, I put my mark on each pot. I claim it as the product of my creative spirit while the clay is still malleable, still in my hands and not quite ready for the final release. With my signature, this pot becomes a part of my legacy to others. I am ready to send it forth from this private place of creation.

The inborn artisan in me is part of my connection with others — a relational dimension of my soul, wanting to make things for others to see and use. Signing my work implies a community that cares and will receive what I am offering. I am aware of some risk and sense of exposure as I imagine others looking at this piece, so the choice to scribe my name or initials into the clay is an act of courage as well.

Claiming my work could be seen as a sign of selfishness, of wanting to "mark my territory," but I see it as an invitation to dialogue and interaction as I take responsibility for my acts of creation in a community of buyers who may or may not be sensitive to my offering. The signature acknowledges both an end to my control and the beginning of new phase, which depends on response by others.

LETTING GO

Once I have finished the basic form, I set this pot with others awaiting the final stages of decoration and firing. This pot no longer has my whole attention. What was unique becomes part of the collective group of pots to be glazed and fired. Later I trust they will be scattered and sold.

"How do you know you'll think of another idea?" one customer asks. My experience tells me more will come. My trust in a deeper source of ongoing creativity is renewed as I finish each pot and put my mark on it. If I have worked a long time on one piece, I may have a twinge of sadness when I remove it from the wheel, but ordinarily I am glad to finish one pot and move on to the next. The rhythm of creation and completion keeps the inner spring of my imagination flowing.

The pots that I build by hand are harder to let go of because they are more personal than pots created on the wheel. Pinched or coiled pots take longer, are more individual, and are more likely to be ritual pots commemorating some significant event. I rarely put a distinctive foot on my handbuilt pots. They seem, rather, to grow out of the supporting surface, like a root out of dry ground. Those pots are still connected to the earth, like a dream or half-formed sentence. They have no distinct beginning because the clay does not have to be centered and opened, nor do they have a distinct foot to end with. Nevertheless, these pots, like all the others, must be finished and set out to dry so I can move on to the next piece.

Finishing something important is never easy. It is a pause in the creative process to replenish and reassess. Wholeness is broken. Unity is scattered. Creativity must have a stopping point or it becomes cancerous. Caring enough to stop making further adjustments is one way of treating death as a normal part of the life process, which we can do if we believe that new life will come. By giving special attention to the ending as well as the beginning, we learn the principal of balance, of ebb and flow. Finishing something is an act of trust in what is past and what is to come, trusting that energy expended will be renewed, trusting our creative impulse enough to embrace endings as well as beginnings, trusting the process enough to pause and wait for something new to emerge. Believing that something new will be born in the place of what has been released is an act of faith!

Journal Questions

1. Close your eyes and imagine yourself walking slowly through your house or apartment. Stop and notice the things that are uniquely you. Open your eyes and list them in your journal, noting what makes each thing special to you.
2. Find a picture of yourself twenty years ago and study the picture. How have you changed? Write about your changes.
3. Name something you have recently let go of to make room for something new. How do you feel about letting go?

GROUP: In your imagination, choose something from your unique possessions that represents something that you have recently let go of or want to release. Then give this imaginary possession to someone in your group, describing it and telling how letting go of this will help you complete a change you are making.

Finishing Stories: Biblical Women

Embracing endings for the sake of new life marks the finishing stories of both the Widow of Zarephath, in the Hebrew Testament, and Priscilla, in the New Testament. Both cared enough about the quality of their own lives to engage in dialogue with male authority figures rather than remain passive. Both claimed the value of their own gifts and were free to share what they had with others. Both let go of what they had known and experienced new life in the process: The widow got her son back because Elijah prayed for a miracle, and Priscilla became a leader in three key locations of the early church: Corinth, Ephesus, and Rome.

The Widow of Zarephath's Story
(I Kings 17:8-24)

I'm going to make this last meal
a celebration for my son and me.
I'll soothe him with stories,
hold him close to my heart,
and hope that our dying will not take too long.
Perhaps I cared for him too much.
As the famine deepened,
I stopped making offerings

to our household gods.
I could not believe it would come to this —
that we would really die.
But I have done all I can.
It is finished now.

I hope he goes first, without too much fear.
I have drawn water while I still have the strength.
My pile of sticks is nearly enough to cook the meal.
Everything is ready for our last supper together.
We will lie quietly here in the shade,
not expend more energy.
Just wait.

What? You, a man of Gilead, ask me for water?
Surely, you can draw water for yourself!
I am only a poor widow, down to our last morsel of food.
My strength is gone. Supplies are short everywhere.
There is no one to care for us.
Surely, you cannot expect me to provide anything for you!

You have no cup?
Then, here, dip your hand in.
It doesn't matter now.
Perhaps you will stay and bury us.

What? You ask me for food as well?
We are down to our last bit of oil and flour!
We cannot share that, too!

You say your God has promised to provide?
New life will come if we share what we have?
How can I be sure?

I can't be?
I must choose?
Well, then . . . I will!
What have I got to lose?

Deciding to share our meal with him began a miracle
I can hardly describe.
Each day there was enough —
like the manna that appeared in the desert
in the Exodus story he told us —
enough for the day and no more.
Cared for and fed.
That miracle was enough to convince me
this man, Elijah, was indeed a prophet of God.

Now we are marked by this manna,
reclaimed from the dustbin of time
by the choice that I made
from my heart.

Would the prophet have found other food?
Was I part of God's plan for this man?
I came close to betraying my past —
denying his gesture of need.
Somehow, from inside,
I felt prompted to give,
and the manna came
for body and soul.

Then my son fell ill.
I could not believe it.
"Have you saved us,
only to let the child die?" I cried.

"What kind of a cruel God would give us life,
only to take my son now?"

Elijah seemed as puzzled as I was.
He claimed that his God could still heal,
but I know the limits of life —
that once we are dead
there's no hope!

Broken and angry, I wailed out my grief
and demanded he leave,
for my life had no meaning,
no purpose at all
without the child's body
to carry my hope for the future.

The prophet just shrugged as I keened my despair,
not able to say what his God was about
but still open to what was ahead — as I wasn't.
I knew the black emptiness sealed up my heart,
but Elijah seemed willing to take a next step.
He cradled my son in his arms
and ascended the stairs
to his room where he prayed,
crying out to his God.

Silence surrounded them there.
I heard not a move,
not a breath, not a word.
Then a sigh.
And the prophet, murmuring prayers,
began the long walk back to where I stood,
silent myself,

but with the tiniest spark deep within.
Could it be?
Could he be . . .?

When the prophet stepped from the shadowy stair
to the silvery light of the moon,
I could see the man burdened,
my child in his arms.

"Mother?"
I wept with gratitude.

Journal Questions

1. What "ritual foods" do you associate with transitions, endings, or celebrations?
2. Where or when do you feel generous and able to share yourself with others?
3. How have you been the recipient of another's hospitality or generosity? What does that mean to you now?

GROUP: Create a "ritual meal" with your group. Bring a simple food to share and take time to tell stories connected with these foods.

PRISCILLA'S STORY

(Acts 18:1-28; Romans 16:3-5;
I Corinthians 16:19; II Timothy 1:16-17; 4:19)

It's good to be back in Rome again,
finished (I hope) with the terrors and trials
of our travels far from here.
Each time we moved,
I felt torn apart, broken into little pieces.

All that I cared about, left behind.
Each place, a new challenge —
a chance to grow in the Spirit.
Many times I wished to be home again,
here on Aventine Hill,
but I never dreamed it would happen.
So much has changed.

At first I didn't recognize the hand of God
in Claudius' edict of '49,
when he ordered all the Jews to leave Rome.
Aquilla knew he would have to go
because he had always supported the synagogue,
but I thought about staying . . .

My family had money and friends in high places.
I guess I was angry and hurt
to be the target of a petty tyrant
when I wasn't even a Jew.

Besides, we had become believers in The Way,
and I hoped God would keep us from harm,
but Aquilla urged me to go with him.
"It's not safe for you either," he said.
"When the Emperor wants to be worshipped as a god,
it's a sign of worse things to come.
Remember, even Jesus was crucified."

But I loved Rome.
Women were expected to be visible,
to own property, to sponsor cultural activities.

I could hold meetings
and invite my friends to learn from visiting teachers
without the least danger or criticism.
I was used to the advantages and tolerance of Rome.
When we talked of going to Corinth,
I was afraid
because I knew that the Greeks did not allow women
such a range of rights.

Over the years, Aquilla's Jewish friends
had been shocked at my education
and my role in our tent-making business,
but I've always enjoyed the challenge of money matters
and been bored by the pastimes of women.
I believe life was meant
for more than primping and preening,
for more than shopping and entertaining others.

So I decided to go with Aquilla to Corinth.
We broke patterns, developed new ways,
because we had to depend so much on each other
in the new places.

Since we were exiled, my faith has changed
from a wispy and wishful kind of hope
to a sturdy dependence on others
who share the communion of Christ.
But when we first left,
I cared too much for the culture I left behind
and couldn't claim the unknown power
yet to come.

The Greek merchants we dealt with in Rome
had always touted Corinth as the cultural heart of Greece,
but when we arrived, I found it provincial,
much smaller and rougher than Rome,
and I had a hard time finding my place there.
Aquilla could go to the synagogue,
but I had no immediate circle of friends.

We found a place to live
at the margin of the merchant quarter,
not nearly as nice as our location in Rome,
but comfortable enough to work in
and convenient for entertaining buyers and suppliers.
Keeping busy was my way of coping with change.

Externally, Corinth provided all the elements
that we wanted:
business opportunities,
a rule of law,
tolerance for religious sects . . .
but internally, I felt the loss
of having no community of women,
and I didn't know where to start.
Without the routines of family and friends,
we were more open to a variety of contacts at work.
That was one benefit of being new.

Now I enjoy our community here
because both men and women
expect to participate, learn, lead . . .
my gifts are as welcome as Aquilla's
and my education valued as much as his.

It's clear to me now
that Jesus did promote a different social order
For women like me,
Jesus was indeed "good news" for us.
He broke tradition
and welcomed the full potential of each person.

Even his view of family was revolutionary.
When he called God "Abba,"
Aquilla says that the Pharisees were appalled,
and the Scribes called it sacrilege.
But for me,
married to a Jewish man
who might have kept me in the kitchen
(or the women's salon),
this Jesus gave me a place
at the table!

I know that, for some married couples,
conversion drove a wedge between husband and wife.
But for Aquilla and me,
it meant discovering a deeper bond.
Our traditional roles in Rome
had already been defined.
Our new sense of partnership
would not have been fully formed
without the shaping we got in the provinces.

When Paul arrived in Corinth,
we met because he was also a tent-maker,
and we invited him to live with us

so we could share expenses and
learn more of The Way from him.
Paul and Aquilla went to the synagogue
for study and discussion,
and I tutored the new believers they brought home.
That in itself was shocking to many:
a woman teaching men!

Widows also flocked to our fellowship
because Paul didn't counsel remarriage,
and soon young married women joined our company, too.
My circle expanded, and I began to feel at home.

When Paul suggested we leave with him for Ephesus,
I was hesitant, but Aquilla was eager to go,
for Ephesus was the primary trading city
between Rome and all of Asia —
a key spot for our business
as well as our mission work with Paul.
But I grieved for the women
I would leave behind.

I decided to follow the example of Jesus
and share a last supper
with each of my friends,
knowing I might never see them again.
I felt the need to claim our circle of friendship
before it was broken and scattered.
Somehow our simple ceremony
made the ending
part of something larger and more lasting.

Ephesus was known as a city of women,
devotees of Artemis ("Diana" to us).
I was both repelled and attracted
by the sight of women coming down
from the temple above the city,
each carrying her lamp —
like a thousand fireflies moving toward the harbor.

Some of the women joined us,
so they could claim their uniqueness
as I had.
As though being tested for more trials ahead,
we were pressured from the very beginning
by the local merchants in Ephesus,
who made a good living from selling statues of Diana.
We taught people to pray to God as Spirit
instead of to a silver statue,
so their business was threatened.
In time, the merchants stirred up so much trouble
that we had to flee for our lives.

Leaving Ephesus was even harder for me
than leaving Corinth
because I knew our work was not finished
and the need was so great,
but I had to trust the Spirit
would complete what we had begun.
When we felt the Spirit calling us back to Rome,
we came, only dimly aware how we ourselves
had been changed.

Now I'm glad to be back.
Our home is still here,
and the number of believers has grown
while we've been gone.
I see the way God has shaped me inside and out
so Aquilla and I can lead the church together.
We've learned to care deeply,
claim our people clearly,
and let each place go when the time has come,
knowing that God will continue to create through us
as long as we are alive.

Journal Questions

1. *If you were suddenly expelled from your home — and you knew your survival needs would be taken care of — what three things would you take with you?*
2. *If you were leaving your present home for a new place and your space was extremely limited, what three things would you leave with regret?*
3. *When you have moved to a new place, what have you done to connect with other people?*

GROUP: Reflect on gifts you are using in this group. Name the gift you are using to encourage this group, allowing time for feedback from the group. Discuss how using your gifts may connect you to the group.

Embracing Endings

Moving from one place to another can be a time of finishing. Often feelings of despair and abandonment come from breaking community ties, but endings can also release unexpected creativity for new beginnings. In 1980, Peter was transferred to Germany while I was in the middle of preparing for the Christmas season and had a studio full of dry pots. We unexpectedly rented our house earlier than we had planned, and I had to clear out space to store our personal belongings. My studio was full of "greenware," finished pots that I had not glazed or fired. There was no time to fire them, and I felt there was nothing else to do but destroy what I had made. Racks of dry bowls, mugs, vases, and teapots had to be disposed of quickly.

On a hot, muggy Saturday in August, I set to this destructive work by myself, though friends had offered to help. I knew it was going to be difficult, and I chose to let myself feel the grief of this death experience without tempering it by my feelings for others. I tipped board after board of finished greenware into large plastic garbage bags, sending up clouds of porcelain dust. Out of my parched throat came howls of anger and sadness while I worked. Death was all around me. Broken dreams, hopeful shapes, beauty gone back to dust.

Finally, just one pot remained. I had made it four years before, coiling it upward by hand until it stood as tall as my kiln: nearly four feet. The base was like wrapped cloth with no distinctive foot. Two small hands and a simplified face peered out of it, watching me while I worked in the studio. I called it my "guardian angel," though it really looked like a papoose with a very small, flat head. I had never had the courage to fire it for fear it would break in the process because it was too large for my kiln.

When I had filled the garbage bags with all the other greenware and set them out on the curb, I turned to my angel pot. I cared about it so much that I could not consign it to the curb with all the others.

No words came, so I sat resting in the dusty desolation, my tears running silently. Conscious of my body, aching now with effort and emotion, I felt spent. Torn. Broken. Scattered without joy or completion. I waited for some inner word to guide me in disposing of this special piece. Something different was needed to finish the work I had started that day, but I could not think what it might be.

Finally, I felt an urge more than a voice. "Let me dissolve in water," it seemed to say, "and return me to the earth."

And that is what I did. I broke my guardian angel pot into pieces and placed them in the water of my hand-washing pail. As I watched the dry pieces soften and begin to crumble, the sharp edges of my resentment and grief began to soften as well. Twenty bags I had taken to the curbside to be taken away by someone else, but I dissolved my angel pot in still water, letting the process take time to return it to the earth from where it first came.

By now, the individual pieces that I put in those garbage bags are long forgotten, but I remember the angel pot clearly. I buried the angel's clay in my garden, an act not unlike scattering the ashes of a loved one for, indeed, that pot looked like the child I never had.

The act of destroying the angel pot felt, as do all finishings, like the border between sexuality and death, between creativity and destruction in my body. If sexuality is the power to love and to create something new in any relationship, no matter how intimate or distant, only death brings that impulse to an end. And finishing marks the turning point between the two. I had given birth to my guardian angel pot, loved her, and then intentionally destroyed her. I knew at some level that I would never return to this work in the form it had been, but as I buried the clay, I trusted that some new form would emerge. That death opened the way to creativity once again; that end, to a new beginning. It was finished, so I could begin another phase of my life.

As I went through the steps of finishing, I went through stages of grief. My caring for the angel pot meant that I was willing to learn from its particular dying process, rather than simply dumping it in a bag with all the rest. Claiming its importance and naming its meaning has let the grief-work continue in my dreams and waking images. Letting go of it had to be done, though the decision was hard: Firing it for posterity was even less of an option on that final day in my studio than it had been before. Dissolving the angel pot was an action that allowed renewal to begin, although I grieved for a long time and did not recognize until recently the healing that happened there. Because I have claimed its meaning for me, I am now able to complete the process of letting go and write this finishing story.

Journal Questions

1. Have you ever finished something by destroying it? Tell the story of that event in your journal.
2. What image or symbol allows you to remember the power and choices involved in that incident?
3. Do you have some further inner work to do around this event? What kind of a ceremony might help you with that?

GROUP: Design a ceremony of finishing or completion (e.g., a burial for a marriage ended or a broken relationship, a graduation for a risk taken and accomplished).

FINISHING AS COMMUNION

Finishing is an act of trust that more will come. It is a basic faith stance of saying "Yes" to our spiritual source, the creative nature of God. And because we are embodied beings, we are saying "Yes" to more than our individual creativity. We are opening to the dynamic of caring in relationship— including our sexuality— between persons of any age or gender.

When we learn to trust that our loving can be renewed, we can claim it fully and let ourselves love deeply, instead of denying our care and concern. Like Priscilla and the Widow of Zarephath, when we have to leave what we have loved in the past, we can claim the relational dimension of our faith to grieve endings as well as claim our hope for new beginnings.

"This is my body, *BROKEN FOR YOU*," Jesus said to his reluctant friends, signaling the end of his time with them on earth. But they did not want the gift of his brokenness; they still wanted him. Ignoring their protests, Jesus divided the bread and passed it to them, scattering the pieces to be eaten and consumed. His body, hidden in their cells by their intentional eating of it. Turned into energy, both physical and spiritual. He invited them to risk the truth of what he was telling them — that they could love him *and* let go of him, that loving one another would be enough to tell the world the true meaning of his life.

As he broke the bread, Jesus also "celebrated" the imminent destruction of his physical body. He knew that finishing meant an end to his bodily presence and the beginning of something new, although the disciples could not imagine what it would be. Jesus' attention to closure helped bring his human life to completion, naming and relinquishing what was past so he — and his followers — could claim what was ahead.

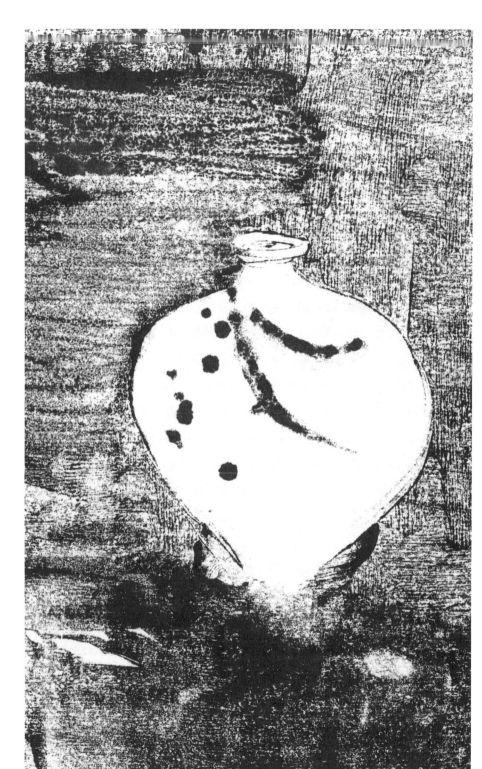

Chapter 6

GLAZING

IMAGINING THE FUTURE

*Glaze is the coating of color
added to bare clay before it is fired.
One method of glazing is to soft-fire the clay first,
then dip the pot in a vat of glaze.
Another method is to brush several coats of glaze
on the raw clay.
Whatever method is used,
glazing requires imagination and experience
to picture the finished product.
Although the basic form does not change,
the dusty appearance of a newly-glazed pot
bears little resemblance to its final luster.*

WHY DOES THE POTTER glaze at all? Why not leave the clay as it is? The answer to that is as old as humankind: We are created with the capacity for play and imagination. We want to do something with a plain surface. The impulse for color and decoration is an essential quality of being human, a quality that we recognize even in the earliest pictures and symbols pressed into clay. We are not confined to living with what we have and what we know. We can envision the future as something different from the present and take steps to achieve it. We have the capacity for vision and creativity even when we do not name ourselves as artists. We can risk and learn from what does not work because we know the source of creation is within. We are created to be creators!

The choices a potter makes during glazing are different from those made in the shaping process because the results of glazing cannot be seen as the color is applied: The color of raw glaze is quite different from the color it will become after it is fired. "Do this and trust your past experience for a probable result" is the potter's guide. She has to rely on her inner eye and give in to the impulse for experimentation.

Like a child who experiences a sense of herself in play, the potter experiences her individuality as she experiments with decoration. With such play, flesh becomes word and takes flight into the future. Glazing and decoration as the capacity for play take us back to the dawn of creation and the very nature of God. Imagination extends time in both directions so we can take risks in the present.

VISION

Unlike the artist who works with paints, which have organic colorants that let the artist see what the finished product will look like, a potter is forced to work with imagination because she works with ground stone. These natural minerals change radically with heat: Chromium pink turns bright green, copper gray turns red, and dull iron browns can have a brilliant metallic sparkle. Learning the chemistry of glaze construction was a surprising doorway for me into the natural world that I had not expected. It provided me with a laboratory experience where spirituality and science could meet with a mystery akin to medieval alchemy.

If shaping a pot means concentrating on the present moment, then glazing gives it a promised future. With my imagination I see the glory of color and decoration as I reach for my brush and choose the basic glaze that will cover the pot. Because unfired glaze does not look at all like it will on the finished product, I need to have an expanded vision and a long time frame in mind when I decide what glaze to use and how it will be applied.

Initially, I look at the shape of a pot to decide how it will be decorated. I nearly always mark the points where the outline makes a strong change of direction, like the foot, shoulder, neck, or lip. Do this or that, the pot seems to say. I then envision how a piece will be used by someone in its final home and imagine a glaze that will fit the intended function. "For you, little mug, a smooth coat of glaze around the rim to make it easy on the user's lip. And for you, elegant salad bowl, a glaze with surface decoration to delight the user's eye when the food is gone. And for you, strange creature, a smooth white slip and lots of bare clay."

RISK

Making choices based on the unseen future is the risky part of glazing. Moving away from functional ware allows the potter to be even more playful and inventive with her vision. Like going to a clothes closet, there are many choices: opaque or transparent, light or dark, thick or thin, rough or smooth, and finally, what basic color(s) and accent(s) are appropriate for this shape or purpose? Many choices and no single right answer, but as with clothing, there are glaze choices that are more appropriate than others to the purpose. Will this glaze make the container watertight? Will that one feel comfortable to the user's hand?

I was trained to choose a glaze that would be functional and beautiful at the same time. My mentor, Louie Mideke, had studied pictures of classic Japanese and Chinese pots, some of them over five thousand years old, and he sought to reproduce those glazes in his studio. He had an unusual process of brushing the glazes on leather-hard clay, using four or five thin coats rather than one thick one that might shrink and separate from the pot's surface. It was a risky procedure, but it gave his pots a quiet luster and depth I have rarely seen elsewhere.

Brushing our glazes on hard clay was uncertain because we knew the clay would shrink up to fifteen percent in the drying process, and the time-consuming process could simply flake off. But Louie worked hard to mix the glazes so they would fit the clay body, with shrinkage factored in, and he was convinced that the glaze formed a tighter bond with the clay during firing as a result.

The risks we took were less apparent because we made them routine. Like walking a tight-rope, we practiced and kept notes until each glaze was known by its idiosyncracies. Some shrank more than others. Some dried more quickly or tended to bond with another glaze more than to the body of the pot. We learned to live with the unknown and did not try to remove all of the variables.

STYLE

Very quickly a potter's method of glazing becomes her signature style in the marketplace. Each person has her own way of working, which develops out of the particular clay body and its glaze covering. Some potters prefer the texture of naked clay, and some, to get variety, mix colorant minerals directly into the body itself. Others cover the clay completely, regarding the body as a surface to be decorated. Because he was working so intensively with a brush, Louie mixed glazes in small amounts and experimented constantly, keeping meticulous records.

My own glazing style grew out of Louie's method of working. I developed three basic glazes and then used my imagination to create combinations with layering for variety. Brushing on layers of glaze also opened up the possibilities for me to use wax to create batik designs on clay. As I stretched my imagination, my eye was naturally drawn to the decorative details in nature. Forms in silhouette worked best: sea grass, bare trees, people dancing against the firelight. My eyes opened to wave patterns on the sand, swirls on shells, and the textures of bark and fern. The incredible variety of patterns and textures I saw in food and field spoke to me of God's creativity and playfulness. Variety seemed to be a sign of health in the organism of nature, and diversity the intent of the Creator! God's extravagant style in nature gave me permission to use wild color combinations, fiddle with texture scratched through the glaze into the raw clay, and even draw graffiti on my pots. "Do this and remember me," the Source of living things seemed to say.

Journal Questions

1. *What kind of clothing are you wearing right now? How does your clothing reflect what you imagined for your day?*

2. *Do you own something to wear that seems risky or out of character? What are the occasions when you wear it? How do you feel in it?*

3. *How would you describe the style of your clothing? What does your clothing generally tell others about you? Imagine yourself in different settings and note in your journal the different "coverings" you choose for those settings.*

GROUP: Bring or wear or describe a "special occasion" garment and tell about the special meaning it has — how you imagine yourself in this garment.

Glazing Stories: Biblical Women

Imagining the future came in very different ways for the Hebrew Testament woman Naomi and the New Testament woman Lydia. Naomi's stubborn faith in the God of Israel bore fruit when her life seemed hopeless: She had the courage to believe, one step at a time. At the end of her story, the women of the village cited her foremothers — Leah, her sister Rachel, and Tamar — to remind Naomi that God works in strange ways, through outcast women, to complete what men sought to control by law and custom. Lydia's faith involved change from success as a woman in business to expanding her future through hosting a house church in Philippi. Both women acted against cultural conventions because they were able to imagine an alternative future.

Naomi's Story
(Ruth 1-4; Matthew 1:5)

Our future closed when my sons died.
We were three women, my sons' wives and I,
all widows, known to be childless.
What man would want us?
Our lives were not worth much in Moab
where the goddess of fertility was worshipped.

But something in me would not die.
I heard that the God of Israel blessed the land
and brought forth food in Bethlehem,
so I decided to return
with or without my daughters-in-law, Orpah and Ruth.
In my dreams and visions,

I saw myself coming home,
to live or to die — it didn't matter which anymore.

They each made a choice.
Orpah, to stay, to return to her mother's house
and hope for a husband in Moab.
Ruth came with me.

"I'll go where you go," she said with her feet,
"and worship your God," she said with lips,
"and die where you die," she said with her heart.
Dreaming a future, leaving her past,
Ruth chose a new world when she came home with me.

But what was the next step after coming home?
I'd learned I had land through Elimelech's line
but knew I couldn't claim it as a woman.
The closest male to inherit it
should have married Ruth to assure us an heir,
but he was more worried about his own line
than ours.

Ruth said she would rather glean for food
than beg for his bed,
so she worked and I prayed.
What more could we do?
Ruth risked her life for me,
and God sheltered both of us.

After noticing Ruth and asking who she was,
Boaz, a more distant kinsman of mine,

told her to stay close to his crew.
At the end of the day,
Boaz gave her a grain gift,
a sign of his care —
and God's protection.
I could see then that God
had covered us both
with strong wings.

It was said that Boaz' mother was Rahab,
the prostitute who sheltered our men
when they hid from the soldiers in Jericho.
Whatever his past, this man understood
both the danger and risk of Ruth's choice,
and he became a symbol of our hope.

I dreamed of the future,
let go of the past,
and trusted that our lives
would be fruitful
at last.

When the harvest was done,
and the barns bulging full,
I knew the men would be celebrating
down at the threshing floor.
"Prepare yourself," I told Ruth,
"bathe and perfume your skin,
dress in your finest robe,
and go down after dark
to the place where Boaz will be resting
slightly apart from his men."

"And then what?" she said with mock surprise.

"Follow his lead, but don't forget
to ask him for this favor:
to redeem us on the morrow."

"Redeem us?"

"Yes. He can go before the council
and offer the property to Elimelech's next of kin,
but if the man is not prepared
to give us an heir by marrying you,
Boaz can ask for you and the property."

"Will he?"

"Yes. His grain gift tells me he is ready.
Now go and prepare yourself."

We did not speak of the danger,
but Ruth knew it full well.
What she had risked in the fields from the men
was deepened by darkness that night.
I could only pray
God would be pouring our future
through Ruth's quick hands
and sure feet.

Ruth did find Boaz in the dark of the night.
He asked who she was
and she answered,
telling him to spread his garment over her
like the wings of God he had wished for her earlier.
As he did so, our risk was resolved.

He acknowledged her loyalty to me
as he agreed to redeem us.
I think Boaz remembered my oldness,
like his own,
when he noted that Ruth
had not sought a younger relative.

The women were wise at the wedding
and sang Ruth the blessings
of Rachael and Leah* —
"May you be mother of many" they meant.

Then the women acknowledged
Ruth's trickery, too:
"Like Tamar you are!" **
Each name from our past was a sign
of how God often used irregular ways
and ingenious women
to birth the possible
into the present.
At the wedding they also warned me to remember Ruth
when her child was born.
Called her a greater gift than seven sons.
Even I was surprised at their truth.

* Genesis 29-30
** Genesis 28

Journal Questions

1. When have you made a difficult choice to be with a friend?
2. Can you recall someone who helped you imagine future possibilities when you could not see them?
3. What image(s) from nature give(s) you hope for renewal? How and when are you in touch with that image?
4. When have you felt guided or supported by God at a risky time in your life?

GROUP: Imagine a "happy ending" for something you are currently struggling with. Who would be there? What would people be saying to you? Rewrite as a role play. Select one or two scenarios from the group to do together.

LYDIA'S STORY
(Acts 16; Philippians 4:3)

We Philippians are a noisy lot.
When I need to replenish myself
after dealing with traders and customers all week,
I like to come away from the city
to this spot by the river.

There is something about moving water — living water —
that draws me to something bigger and deeper than myself,
something formless, but powerful.
Not the super-human gods of my Greek friends,
but a mysterious lifeforce beyond those gods —
perhaps the "One God" I have heard Jews speak of.

As a Greek, my heritage seems to be split in two parts,
body from spirit.
When I come here to the river,

I leave my physical cares behind and go inward,
to darkness and peace
beyond words, beyond things,
toward the Source.

I know something in me
is wanting to speak,
wanting a form in the world.
But I can't quite see what it is.
Whatever draws me to the water
wants more union of body and spirit.
I know that much.
Some call it soul.
Others just laugh
and say I'm a dreamer.
I come here often to listen,
to learn from the living water.

I was at the river with some friends
talking of these spiritual matters,
when three men approached
and asked if they could sit down with us.
I could tell they were Jewish by their accent,
though I could understand their Aramaic perfectly well.
As a dealer in purple, my travels have taken me
all around the Mediterranean,
even to Jerusalem.

But I was surprised when they asked to sit down.
Think of it — Jewish men —
asking to join us, Greek women!
At first I was irritated to be interrupted,

but they seemed different from other men.
At home here, by the river.
They seemed at ease and made no move to leave.

After a few minutes of polite exchange,
our talk returned to spiritual matters.
They told us that they no longer worshipped
at the temple in Jerusalem,
though they still obeyed the Law.
But I could see they had been liberated
from some of their legalistic restrictions
because here they were, talking with us!

They told us the promised One, the Messiah,
had already come — and gone.
That he had been killed,
crucified like a common criminal.

Could not a Messiah avoid death? I thought.
Would the One God let him die,
like an ordinary man?
But I continued to listen.
And then they said that this man
(Jesus, they called him)
had come back
(as the Christ, they then said) —
that they had seen him
and touched him and eaten with him.

As I listened,
I could feel it inside.
The real me, I would call it.
More than a dealer in purple.

More than a dreamer by the river.
Some part that was buried
was coming to life.
As they spoke,
my soul danced,
asking for more.

When I spoke of the Spirit,
Paul, their leader, acknowledged the sign
and offered to baptize me and my household in the river.
I felt cleansed and claimed and made new.

It was too much for one day,
so I invited them to stay with us
and teach us more about their new understanding.
I felt Paul was giving me words for something
I'd really known for a long time:
That we are all connected.

I suspect that's why my business thrives.
I call it care . . .
for customers and competitors alike.
I began to see some applications
for women who wanted a spiritual life
beyond business or making a home.

Paul stretched my imagination even further
when he spoke of the Spirit
poured out on all people, young and old,
male and female, slave and free,
but I found it disturbing when he said finally,
"We are all meant to be servants."

That's what my business frees me from, I thought.
I'm nobody's servant, nobody's wife.
I choose where I go, who I meet, what I want.
My independence matters most to me.

Over time, though, I began to see a different future,
another way of working:
Sharing our talents and our resources
to include the more vulnerable ones.
My house became a refuge
for some of the young women
who didn't want to marry.
And for widows
who refused to be passed on with their property
to the next male in their husband's family.
We began to create an ongoing community.
With regular worship. Cooperative living.
Care for the aging . . . and for the children
who were homeless in our neighborhood.

I really didn't notice the change,
but the style of my life was shifting
from making money
to caring for the good of us all.
Not that I left my own business,
but rather I included others
in my plans for the future,
and I stopped traveling so much
because my community needed my leadership
in person.
From Christ in our midst,
I was learning the power of being personal.

Women were beginning to make their own decisions
because of our Christian community,
and that made some men angry.
Merchants and princes began to see
their ability to make political alliances through marriage
eroding.

I began to notice hostility among traders
who had formerly been willing to deal with me.
Perhaps I should have seen the conflict coming
because I know human nature well
and have seen the dark side of greed often enough.
But their opposition took me by surprise.

I think some of the powerful merchants
were looking for an excuse
to pressure us into disbanding our community,
because when Paul healed a slave girl
and the owners lost her spiritual powers,
a riot erupted against us!

We barricaded ourselves in the house
and sent word for other Christians to stay away.
That night, I served at the communion table
because death seemed so near.
"Do this," I could hear,
so we did.
And it helped.

The riot tested our faith as nothing else had.
I remembered the stories of Jesus and the cross

and was not sure we could withstand trial or torture.
But we were spared.
And so were Paul and Silas, safe in jail,
though the earthquake unlocked all the doors.
They returned to us briefly
after they were released, but soon left
saying the Spirit was calling them on.

Now I'm left to lead a church
toward whatever future God is giving us.
Two sacraments we have to guide us:
Baptism lets the river of Spirit
run through us for others, and
Eucharist helps us live
past fears of death.
"Do this," the Spirit says,
and so we are sustained.

Journal Questions

1. Where do you go to nurture your spirit?
2. Have you ever been afraid for your life or your lifestyle? Describe this time in your journal.
3. Whom would you contact if a friend or mentor of yours had been arrested? What other help have you discovered in an emergency?

GROUP: Think of some way to honor the person who called this group together for her vision and initiative.

Shadows of Hope

Imagining the future is difficult when one receives an ultimatum. A doctor's diagnosis in 1980 sharply changed my direction, forcing me to take a risk no matter which way I decided to respond. I became conscious for the first time of my body's vulnerability. While clay had awakened my whole body and breath with a thrilling kind of aliveness and creativity, the words, "It looks like ovarian cancer," felt like a death sentence. Was my body was destroying life from the inside out? Should I try some alternative method of healing? All my instincts resisted having surgery. "Do this or die," was what I heard.

Because the doctor felt we ought to act quickly, I don't remember much personal denial . . . except I didn't ask Peter to come back from Europe for the surgery nor did I tell my parents. Of course, I see the denial now. I was trying to keep my external relational structures in place with some fantasized effect that perhaps my internal organism would conform! I wanted the outside centering hand to contain my fear so my inner sense of self would not collapse. That is not what I believe, but it is what I did.

Between the tests and the surgery, I went to a Faith at Work women's retreat as part of the leadership team. I do not remember speaking about my Monday morning date at the hospital. I tried to minimize the risk by continuing my routines. I kept the words inside because I could not bear to say them, even to myself.

I could not face my fears or share the shame I felt: My own body was betraying me! Until then, I had taken my body's health and strength for granted. I had hardly ever been sick. I counted on my endurance, laughed about my hardy Dutch heritage, didn't bother with external appearances much.

I have almost no memory of that Women's Event except for a guided meditation in which we were asked to picture Mary, the mother of Jesus. My mind called up Michelangelo's Pieta at St. Peter's in Rome, but instead of the young Christ across her lap, I saw myself, vulnerable and weak as a dying child. Suddenly, I was on Mary's lap, sensing her presence close to me, hearing her crooning voice as I felt the slight rocking motion of her body all around me. "I will stay with you," she said softly.

When the leader encouraged us to write a dialogue with Mary in our journals, I wrote this:

> *I will stay with you.*
> I'm terrified!
> *I will stay with you.*
> Am I'm going to die? Has it spread?
> Why didn't I tell Peter? Or my parents?
> *It doesn't matter now. Let go of your fears.*
> *I will stay with you.*

That was Sunday morning, before the closing worship of the retreat, but I still did not share my fears with the team.

My tension increased on Sunday evening when my friend Marianne took me to the hospital, and we learned that the tests did not look encouraging. I signed the necessary release forms for the doctors to take out whatever diseased parts they found, and Marianne arranged for me to move from a ward to a private room because there would probably be a longer recovery time than I had first thought.

Then she left the hospital to return shortly with communion elements. We had a "last supper" together. "This is my body . . .," I said ruefully, as the knowledge of what Jesus faced that dreadful night sank into my soul. My body. Broken. Yes. Do this . . . . Do what? Break bread? Pray for healing? Trust Mary? Ask for a miracle? All of the above? None of the above?

Marianne prayed with me, guiding me back to my dialogue with Mary from the retreat. By the time she left, I was ready to live with whatever lay ahead. The vision of Mary was enough. I promptly fell asleep.

That night I had a dream that gave me hope. I was driving a little car along a dark street in a city when I heard a high-pitched scream. I drove my car through a basement window, into a lighted office where nobody seemed to hear the scream. When I asked about it, somebody directed me to a back room, where the scream seemed to be coming from behind a brick wall. I unbricked the wall, and inside was a dinosaur who stopped screaming as I let it out.

When I drew the scene in my journal, I noticed that the dinosaur looked like a uterus with a long neck and had a worn-out tennis shoe for a head. I took the dream to mean that my womb was extinct, my ovaries useless, and they needed to be released from my body. That vision of the future made my waiting possible.

I went into surgery with a sense of Mary all around me and the humorous imagery of the dream as a sign that part of my body was screaming for release. The first sound I heard as I came out of the anesthetic was the voice of Mary humming a lullaby, as though I had been held and rocked in her arms the entire time. A few days later, as I looked at the ugly wound sutured by twenty-seven staples marching politely from belly-button to crotch, the doctor reported there had been very little bleeding, the cancer was in an early stage and had not spread, and I could expect a full recovery.

. . . Except for the scar in our lives where children might have been. That was not so easy to heal. When I got to

Germany three weeks later, I was aware of being numb and feeling neutered. Sexless. Robbed of the image we had of a choosing whether or not to have children. I felt as shapeless and formless as raw clay once again.

Because I no longer had a pottery studio in which to work out my grief and recover my soul, I began writing instead. Peter borrowed an electric typewriter that would work on German current, and I started letting the words take shape like clay, kneading the images, centering and recentering short pieces like a child learning to crawl again. I started writing a series of conversations with my inner guide, Mary, which I called "Confessions of a Protestant Daughter." The writing helped me recover my power to name my experience, even though the words were rough and not intended for anyone else to read.

At the same time, I was learning to breathe again by singing with a group. I wasn't ready to share my story yet, but I did want to belong to a group where I would be missed if I was gone. First, I joined a women's chorus, and that led to a women's barbershop quartet. All I needed to do was to learn the music and do my part.

So I put in the time each day. Though the results did not match my ideals, somehow the discipline I learned in the pottery studio was enough to keep me going. "Just do it," I would tell myself, "even though you don't feel inspired, even though you don't know what it will lead to." Gradually, my creativity began to find its way onto the page and into my voice. As the wellspring of my spirit began flowing again, I began to dream of finding a network of people who wanted to share a journey of creativity and change. More and more of my writing was focused on biblical women. I had a shadowy intuition that they could help me reclaim my feminine sense of self.

During the two years that we were in Germany, I began to envision a different future that would give us a different kind of family, a chosen family of faith. By the time we moved back to Washington D.C. in 1982, I was ready to risk again: I applied for admission to Virginia Theological Seminary. By then, I also knew my style of ministry would be different from the traditional route of completing the requirements of an institutional system, so I entered as a special student and began to explore the different ways I might glaze the living pot of my life.

Journal Questions

1. *If you are aware of a risk or major question that you are facing now, take time to breathe and relax. Then let a wisdom figure (like Mary) come to you. Write down your conversation with that figure.*

2. *Does a vision for the future emerge from your conversation? If so, what is it? If not, introduce into the conversation a question about your future.*

3. *Make a series of pictures in which you focus on color, not shapes, to observe the direction of your imaginary conversation.*

GROUP: Share with your group, in whatever way you choose, one of your color studies from your conversation with the wisdom figure.

GLAZING AS COMMUNION

The point of glazing is not to eliminate risk but to learn trust and allow our natural capabilities for imagination to emerge. When we give ourselves permission to entertain new possibilities, even ones that seem unlikely, we have begun to recover a capacity for play and imagination that all of us had as children. Out of body action, a word or picture can emerge as a guide to the future until cognitive understanding fills in the details. Just as Naomi offered her vision to Ruth, and Lydia helped her followers believe in the future, imagination can help us turn terror into story and trust the creative source within us.

As Jesus prepared his disciples for his death, he gave them a ritual of bread and wine, saying simply "*DO THIS* in remembrance of me." When he said "Do this," he was commanding the disciples to celebrate Passover in a new way. Not to expect the angel of death to pass over this house, as the ancient Passover ritual did, but to invite the dreaded guest of death to their table. To befriend the enemy, trusting in a transformation they could not see. He gave them an image and a ritual so their own actions would carry them beyond his physical presence.

Even though the disciples could not imagine what the bread and wine might have to do with helping them live into a future without Jesus, he gave them something specific to do, offering them his imagination and his vision as a guide. The disciples had to trust that the word-action would open their future once again.

Because Jesus' vision was larger than theirs, he knew that the shared ritual of the Last Supper would continue to give them an image of wholeness and possibility as their understanding came. Jesus remade the Passover ritual from God's promise to a people into a personal encounter with the very Source of life itself. Not a set of rules, or a moral code, or even power to heal the sick. They had already done those things. In the end Jesus gave them a simple meal with a new meaning as his act of trust for the wisdom needed to live into dying. "Do this, and it will help you through a process you do not understand." He knew that the ceremony could be repeated for many generations, touching their pain and ours with mystery and the possibility of transformation.

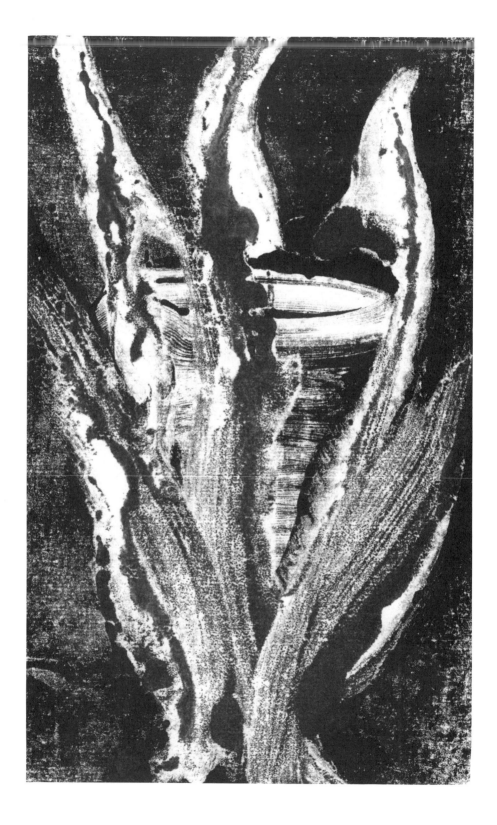

Chapter 7

FIRING

TRUSTING THE OUTCOME OF CHANGE

Loading the kiln is holy work.
Each shelf is stacked carefully
with pots of a similar height.
The kiln is sealed,
and heat is applied with gas or electricity
until the ware inside is translucent.
Firing changes the form and substance
of both the clay and glaze,
creating a new crystalline structure
as the original molecular mixture melts and changes,
bonding clay and glaze.
Slow cooling completes the process.
Unloading the kiln is like discovering a treasure every time!

FIRING TOUCHES something primal in me. I am attracted by the fire's warmth and dancing light, but instinct tells me to pull away when fire gets too close because I know it burns, consumes, and kills live tissue. That is, indeed, what happens to the clay: Organic matter burns away and only stone, so dense and thin that it rings like a chime, is left.

Firing leaves no room for indecision. I must commit the pots I love to the fire's consuming power without recourse to rescue if something unexpected happens. Waiting for the heat to do its work is a discipline born of experience.

Remembering past results and my hopes from the glazing process help me take the time necessary for the fire to complete the process I have started. There are no shortcuts. We finally must see our commitment through to the end.

The prize for this commitment is transformation — a new internal structure — but to get that I must let go of my control and trust change to a power greater than my own. Firing pots comes close to making things "immortal," with all the awe and terror of coming face to face with God.

COMMITMENT

When I have only a few pots and want to get them through the process, I feel poor, and I am anxious that the firing turn out well. But when I have enough pots to choose the optimum combination for each shelf, I feel rich and full, ready to commit some portion of my store to the transforming heat of the kiln. The empty chamber waits, pristine with a coat of kiln-wash to keep runny glazes from sticking. When I am ready to let go of what my hands have made and trust the fire to do its work, I begin to sort the pots by size. Loading the kiln is always an act of willingness to accept the outcome, whatever that may be.

Both anticipation and anxiety hover around the loading process as I examine each pot to make sure there is no glaze on the bottom rim, which would fuse it to the shelf inside the kiln. I check the glaze coat to make sure there are no bare spots where the glaze dried away from the clay and dropped off, no chips or cracks that would guarantee failure. Each pot gets this final inspection as I place it close to the others of similar height for best heat conduction. There is something comforting about the closeness of these pots,

as if they stand together before some fearsome threat —
for radical change always flirts with extinction.

As I load each shelf, I place three stilts on that shelf to
hold the next higher one, and I repeat the process of loading
another shelf until the kiln is full. Many kilns have room to
stack four or five shelves this way, one on top of the other.
If the shelves are warped with many firings, or if the stilts
have picked up a bit of grit or kiln-wash so they do not stand
absolutely straight, the stack of shelves can be precarious.
Taking care with stacking the kiln is a ritual of preparation,
methodical and precise, doing what I can do to make the
firing successful.

Then I place three cones in a pad of clay and set them
where I can see them through a peephole in the wall of the
kiln. Made of specially-mixed clay to melt at specific tem-
peratures, the cones are a better measure of heat applied
over time than a mechanical thermometer would be. Once
I have checked to make sure the cones are visible, I brick
up the door, sealing the pots inside so the firing chamber
acts like part of the chimney. Preparing the kiln reminds me
how often routines and risk go hand in hand.

WAITING

Once again, the temptation to hurry must be tempered, and
I light the burners for a low heating period to drive off any
remaining surface water. At two-hundred and twelve degrees, the point at which water turns into steam, glaze can
"pop off" and damp pots can explode. I hold the temperature
near this boiling point, checking for surface steam with a
mirror held to the peep hole, and when no more water
condenses on the mirror, I begin to push the temperature
upward more rapidly.

At first the firing is pure sound: Gas burners roar, like a propane torch. The kiln is pitch-dark inside. Then an orange glow begins to appear as the pots heat up. As more heat is applied, the color in the kiln changes to bright yellow and, finally, to a white heat. By this time, day has turned to night, and the whole kiln glows and roars in the darkness.

When the temperature climbs over two-thousand degrees Fahrenheit, I reduce the oxygen by closing the burner ports, while still allowing enough air in to keep the fire hot enough for chemical change to happen throughout. Reducing the oxygen affects both color and crystal development of the soft and viscous glazes. Tongues of flame reach for air out of every crack in the kiln, and the kiln has the look of a devouring dragon, reaching for air to keep its fury going. In this final stage the kiln has its own fiery soul and its own timing for the work of change taking place inside.

Like a sentry posted to guard and yet still encourage the dragon's breath, I watch through the peephole until all three cones melt flat, telling me that the chemical change in clay and glaze has been completed. Then I turn off the burners, block the ports so cool air cannot crack the pots, and seal the other openings. My long vigil is over. I am often exhausted and glad to sleep when a firing is finished.

Just as I have waited for the pots to heat, I now must wait again to see what the fire has done. Slow cooling is probably as important as heating in the formation of a new substance. From a translucent and nearly liquid state, the clay and glaze must re-stabilize without cracking. The discipline of waiting is an act of remembering what I have learned from practice; waiting stands like a silent word from nature against the pressure for instant results. I learn again that transformation takes time!

RELEASE

Finally, it is time to open the kiln, to release the pots from their chamber of change. As I unbrick the door, light enters and sparkles on jeweled surfaces, showing green, blue, red, gold, and white where before there had been only chalky dust. The pots are still warm as I cup each one in my hands, examining each piece like a newborn child. It is the miracle of Christmas morning every time!

As I stand in the cool morning air, warmed by the kiln while the firebrick continues to give off heat, I remember my hopes for each special glaze and look for results. Sometimes I am surprised, for the unexpected blush has marked this one with a unique beauty or that one with a blemish I must accept. No matter how often I fire, opening the kiln is like rolling away the stone and experiencing resurrection first-hand!

Journal Questions

1. Where are you being "tested by fire" ?
2. If you are waiting for something in your life to change, how long do you expect to wait? What will the signs of readiness be?
3. What intentional commitments have you made in the recent past? To or for your body-self? To primary relationships? To your work?

GROUP: If you are being "tested by fire" in some area of your life, share some of the transitional elements you are aware of.

Firing Stories: Biblical Women

Firing requires trust and courage, as well as skill and practice, to complete the process of transformation. Hannah had it and so did Mary Magdalene. Both let themselves be transformed by the heat of their love for another — changed to the point where they could release the beloved one to his own destiny. For Hannah, weaving a coat for her son became a yearly sign of her pledge to release him. For Mary Magdalene, the choice to "not hold on" but to "go and tell" marked the transition from being a disciple to being the first evangelist of the early church. Both women were transformed by love.

Hannah's Story
(I Samuel 1; 2:1-11, 18-21)

I long for a child.
Not just to please Elkanah —
God knows he has been more than loving to me
even though I haven't borne him a child —
but for myself.
To fulfill my purpose in being.

Elkanah's other wife, Penninah, has many children,
so our family future is assured,
but my body burns with longing
to bear one of our own.

Elkanah tries to comfort me —
"Am I not more to you
than ten sons of your womb?" he asks,
but he is no substitute for the creator I want to be.

Every year we go to Shiloh
to offer sacrifices of thanksgiving to God,
to remember our deliverance from Egypt,
to hear Eli, the priest at Shiloh, preach and teach.

I made a vow at Shiloh:
I will give the child to You
if You will open my womb!

The priest thought I was drunk!
"Put away your wine!" Eli said,
because I was praying with my lips
but making no sound.
Think of it. A priest who could not tell I was praying!
What else would I be doing at the altar?

But Eli cared enough to listen
when he spoke to me of drinking,
and he heard my deep longing for a child
when he asked what was troubling me.
He gave me his blessing
for the vow I had made before God.
Promised to pray with me.
Told me he would receive my child when it came
and care for it like a father.

Secretly, I thought God might send me a little girl.
Then she could stay home with me after all.

But the child was a boy.
We named him Samuel,
which means, "I have asked for him from God."

When it was time for us
to make our next yearly pilgrimage to Shiloh,
I decided to stay at home until the child was weaned.
"Do what seems best to you," Elkanah said,
and he took Penninah and her children with him.

Elkanah wrapped us in his love
when he did not insist that we go,
leaving us to savor one more year together.
I loved sharing the silence with little Samuel.
I held him and talked with him
and knew his body was part of my own,
filled with joy.

When Samuel was finally weaned,
we took him to Shiloh with a brand new coat
just big enough for him to grow for a year.
So young. So small.
Will he be all right? Have enough to eat?
Have someone to cover him at night?
Hold him when he cries?
Laugh as he learns something new?
I think of him all the time.

As I spin the wool for his coat,
love pours through my fingers
touching each thread, twisting them together,
until the whole garment is made of my heart.

Each year I take him a new coat
as my offering of love.

It is a garment shaded with grief for my first-born,
a raiment of remembering.

Each year it is different.
My body holds the pain of our separation
like a kiln
roaring with fire,
transforming my tears
into love
so I can let him go
again.

Since Samuel left our home,
God has blessed us with more children:
three sons and two daughters,
but none can replace the empty space
where I hold Samuel
in my heart.

Journal Questions

1. *What longing has led to commitment in your life?*
2. *What sign of your major commitments do you wear or have in your home?*
3. *What major commitments have you relinquished to a "transforming fire," either by choice or accident?*

GROUP: On a coat or similar outer garment, arrange items that represent commitment from all members of the group. Gather in a circle around the collection in silence, looking carefully at each one. Then let anyone so moved speak of her commitment to the group.

MARY MAGDALENE'S STORY
(Luke 8:2; Mark 15:40-47;16:1-9; John 20:1-18)

We all knew the risk.
Going to Jerusalem was dangerous.
Too many leaders saw Lazarus raised.
Too many ordinary people caught sight of God's nearness.
Jesus cared too much, couldn't keep quiet.
And couldn't stay away.
So all of us went from Bethany to Jerusalem
to celebrate Passover together,
like family,
hoping once more
that the angel of death
would pass by.

On the outside, it was fine.
You couldn't tell what was coming.
The people gave him a palm procession, like a king!
A people's king — common — rising up out of the masses
like one of them.
People cheered and crowded around, crying "Hosanna!"

But when he went to the Temple
and began scattering the money-changers and merchants,
we knew trouble had come . . .
He was touching their holy symbols,
scattering their gods!
Money! Power! Position!

"This is my Father's house!" he thundered. "Get out!"
His face was aflame with fury. His voice like a whip.

Some thought he was crazy, out of his mind.
Afraid he had gone berserk.
But I knew his anger came from another source.
I saw him alive with God.
Transparent in the heat of his passion.
Daring their hate with his hands.

"This is my Father's house!" he screamed!
"This is my Body," he sobbed.
And it was all the same.
No more temple. No more ritual. No more distance.
Abba as close as body and breath.
As close as life itself.

Then the full shape of his message came clear.
No one thought of God as Father.
So familiar. So close. Not Abba.
At Passover, of all times.
No wonder the priests were so full of hate.
He was breaking their hold.
Taking their gods.
Giving the people a key
to unlock the Holy of Holies.

Later, in the upper room, as we shared Passover together,
he recalled the Exodus, held up the unleavened bread,
and shocked us again by making the link
between his body and our Body, holy and whole.

"This is my body, broken for you.
Do this in remembrance of me."

Passover changed forever, though we didn't know how.
Our slavery ended.
Worship returned to the table.
So close. So common. So clear.

He spoke of his body, looking at us.
"Remember . . ." he said.
And we would.
How could we forget?
Seared in our hearts, he brought God right up close.

Then the angel of death knocked,
and Judas left quickly.
It happened so fast.
Some fled, too afraid to face the fury of the crowd.
Some stayed, locked in the upper room.
We were scattered by our own fears,
for we were not yet his Body.
Not yet transformed ourselves.

My feet wouldn't leave.
I stayed close by the cross,
hearing him gasp
and let go.

Now my feet feel the road where his feet walked.
My breath takes in the breath he breathed out.
My heart holds his sigh.
"It is finished," he said,
like the end of a race.

I went to the tomb before dawn,
dying myself.
Dragging my heart.
Over and over, beginning and end.
Body broken. Scattered. Waiting forever.

Then a shape formed through my tears. A man . . .
"Sir, tell me where you've taken him," I asked.

"Mary," I heard.

What? Not gone? Here still? How?
My heart split wide open!
I reached out, blindly groping.

"Mary, don't hold on to me.
I haven't yet gone to my Father."

Could I hold him? Keep him here?
Was he saying I could? But should not?
How could I bear not to touch him again?

"Go and tell my disciples what you have seen and heard."

Was I going mad? Crazy?
Would they believe me?
They'd already seen the tomb empty.
Could he be here, alive?

Love leaped between us, like a flame.
The curtain of death torn in two
by my name in his voice.

Released.
To return to the living.
So I turned
toward the future
alone.

Journal Questions

1. *Have you gone someplace "while it was yet dark" in a desperate attempt to bridge some gap between yourself and a loved one? Recall the details and write that story in your journal.*
2. *When has someone "called you by name" in such a way as to awaken your soul? If you haven't been "called" in this way, can you imagine such a call?*
3. *If you need to "turn away" from something in order to move to the next stage of your life, how might that happen?*

GROUP: Add to the assemblage on the coat (see the Group Question on page 173) a candle and enough stones for each person. Then do a simple ritual of transition by beginning with your name and a statement of new intention for the future. Pick up a stone to symbolize your commitment.

TRIED BY FIRE

As a woman, I have often felt my loyalties divided between work and family. In some ways work has been the outer pressure and home, the container for my inner life. After my surgery in 1980 and Peter's retirement from the Army in 1982, I had an opportunity to focus on my work in a new way. Peter was clear about his intention to support whatever outer expression of my inner work I wanted to do. I was not so clear what that could be, except to acknowledge that my soul held the key to what I wanted to offer others. My body had healed sufficiently to feel balanced and pliable again. My spirit felt restless and ready to fly, ambitious and angry about the delay. My inner world, where body and spirit meld as clay, was in flux once again, as we moved into this new phase of both marriage and work.

1983 was a kneading and needing time. By the time we had moved from Germany back to Washington, D.C., I had been away from my pottery studio for two years. The unity I had felt from working at home in my pottery studio was gone. I had begun writing as a form of therapy and inner healing, and had also developed an informal network of contacts for offering church renewal events. All of the pressures seemed to be coming from outside. I had no clear sense of inner space or inner shape. My soul felt soft and moist, but still nameless and formless. Volunteer work as coordinator of women's ministry for Faith at Work offered a framework for my interest in spiritual growth. I began to consider professional work in a church-related ministry and entered seminary the following year.

School became the centering outside hand while my spirit hovered over the new possibilities, looking for the perfect job, scanning the horizon. It was hard for me to settle down and let my soul take shape in the real world again. Peter and my community at The Church of the Saviour also helped to contain my spirit and keep me from "flying into space" as I began to travel and design biblical learning events. My soul began to feel centered and ready again.

In retrospect, I think my spirit wanted the power of being a priest, but my soul was seeking a more ordinary form. Something more down-to-earth. Speaking in the vernacular. Working with my hands. But my spirit was pushing for more. I felt ambivalent about seeking ordination and noticed that I was drawn to rebels and dreamers in the institutional church. Seminary was a place to sort that out.

Moving from a volunteer to a paid status at Faith at Work supported my seminary studies and helped me regard my interest in spiritual matters more seriously. One major advantage of my new position was the travel associated with doing retreats: It symbolized my independence and gave me a way to see my parents, who were a continent away. During that time, the kneading continued. My father was making some radical adjustments to life with colon cancer, and I made a number of trips across country, from Washington, D.C. to Bellingham, Washington, to be with him through surgery and chemotherapy.

The grounding that my father provided in our family was softening, settling earthward, and we often talked of the hope he was finding in the cycles of nature as he worked the soil on his holly farm outside Bellingham. As his body became more vulnerable, I wanted to provide some refuge and support for him. I found new tenderness in my words and interaction with him and with others. Being with him several times a year during the period from 1983 to 1987 gave me space to be an ordinary companion, going to the farm with him and, in the evenings, playing through the hymn book as he rested. My soul was at peace during those times, doing small and simple things to make him more comfortable. Being with him helped to heal my feelings of rejection and loss because I could not have children. This grounding and kneading prepared me for a change in my work.

Centering my soul work outside of home required models at first. My imagination was quickened by two men who seemed to embody the kind of ministry I wanted. One was Wes Frensdorf, the Episcopal Bishop of Nevada. The other was Michael Vermillion, the priest who had earlier blessed Frieda, my clown, and had encouraged the spiritual dimension of my work with clay. With both of them, I talked about the question of whether I should seek ordination to become a "real" priest. I realize now that I was testing my need for a father's approval and finding my own form of faith and community. Both men were interested in my career choices and helped me to articulate the questions I needed to ask.

I began to feel centered and sure that I wanted some form of ministry, though I was not ready to leave The Church of the Saviour for a mainline denomination. Wes invited me to give summer workshops at Lake Tahoe and talked with me about his "total ministry" program for ordaining local leadership in small congregations. Michael welcomed my workshops to nurture people in his parish, where they offered to sponsor me if I wanted to start the ordination process.

Shaping my soul work had both an inner and outer dimension. When I became president of Faith at Work in 1985, I left seminary and had an opportunity to experiment with forms of ministry that the traditional church did not offer. Creative inner work pressed against routine administrative demands to form a unique vessel. The way opened for additional teamwork with both of my church mentors. I traveled with Wes through Navajoland, where he had become the Bishop, and I saw his radical vision — based on the model of the first-century church — taking shape with indigenous leaders there. I used my potter's wheel to preach when we had no interpreter, and I still have a green cornmeal communion wafer given to me by an old Navajo woman when I gave her the rest of my clay at the end of our trip. With Michael, who was located much nearer in Virginia

Beach, I shared my writing and theological reading as we developed a mutual support relationship by phone and mail. Those opportunities shaped my soul and vision for ministry.

Within Faith at Work, finishing was an ongoing process of completing many small projects, like a potter throwing many pots. Running an office on a tight budget with volunteer helpers around the country clarified the choices I needed to make. For every creative impulse from my heart, there were two "ought to's" and three "should's" that simply had to be done. As I took care of finishing the foot (our financial base) and the lip (our national magazine), I did not know how important it would be to claim my role in Faith at Work as a form of ministry at the growing edge of the Church and let go of formal ordination in a denomination.

The glazing stage began as I used my imagination to create two books around the edges of my job. *Braided Streams* and *Seasons of Friendship* were both based on women's stories from the Bible, and they included journaling questions that came out of my soul-making journey. Although they are not academic or scholarly, I continue to be surprised and pleased by their acceptance by a wide-ranging audience of people working alone and in small groups. Writing these books was a another new form of ministry at my growing edge!

Then, suddenly, the firing time came in 1987. First, Wes was killed in a small plane accident in the Grand Canyon. Then Michael died in a car accident that summer. And, finally, my father died at home with hospice help in the Fall. The men who had carried the shape of my inner life in the world were suddenly gone. It felt as though the organic matter, the living form that they provided, had been burned away, and now I was left with the fired clay of my own soul.

In the three days I had between my father's death and his memorial service, I wrestled with the Scriptures he had wanted me to use — the last verses of Ecclesiastes. I thought they expressed only his Calvinist doctrine of judgment, not the faith that had allowed him to live fully into death. I paid attention to my dreams, looking for an image of the grace that I had felt growing in his life, but which we had never discussed. On the last night, the right image came: A cherry tree in full blossom at the farm. He had used a photo of this tree on his last Christmas card with these words: "Spring snow at Eastertide." Birth and death. Baptism and Eucharist. I knew then he had reached resurrection on his soul-making journey, and I could tell the story with a sense of releasing him to the future. As I spoke, I was releasing myself as well. As I described his Christmas/Easter image, I found my voice in the pulpit — like the ring of a high-fired bowl after a good firing.

The firing time in 1987 released me from looking for my father's blessing in male authority figures and helped me to turn away from these substitutes for my own soul making. I found new commitment and resolve to claim my perspective as a woman. I am learning to wait until guiding images come from inside, and I feel hopeful about living into each firing period.

Journal Questions

1. Reread the journal entries that you have written as you were reading this book.
2. Notice examples of your own creativity and ability to live with change. Mark those or list them separately.
3. Color an image of your creative self.

GROUP: *Share your image of who you are now with your group. Thank the other members of the group and say "Good-bye," releasing each other for your soul-making process.*

FIRING AS COMMUNION

Being transformed by the fire of commitment is a process that changes us, as it changed both Hannah and Mary Magdalene. We learn to release the beloved and be released at the same time. When tested by fire, we learn to love without needing possession or control. We can re-member the relationship by choice rather than being bound by it unconsciously.

"This is my body, broken for you," Jesus said at the Last Supper, "Do this *IN REMEMBRANCE OF ME.*" He gave his disciples a ritual to hold on to as they entered the fire themselves. Their commitment to care had been forged by the choice they had made to join Jesus in the first place, as well as the time they had spent together in many different situations. They had much to remember, but no experience in how to be One without Jesus to guide and direct them.

The question they must have carried into the firing time of his death on the cross was how they could re-member his body. Even though he had told them not to be afraid, that his Spirit would come as their counselor and teacher, they could not know what he meant until they had experienced it themselves, in the flesh. As they sat around the table, eating the unleavened bread, they could only hope for the internal change that would be necessary to re-member themselves as his Body — and perhaps worry about the weaknesses they knew so well.

"Re-member me," he said. Bring the parts back to-gether. Do not despise or exclude one another. Let your-selves be intimate with your pain and joy. Do not hold back from touch or footwashing. Take on the role of a servant to one another. In all these actions, you re-member me.

Jesus released his disciples from their bondage to the past by transforming the Passover ritual into promise and hope for the future. He changed a common meal with his Being and his words, giving them the power to do the same. Familiar as the family dinner table. Sacred as the soul he shared so openly.

Remember me this way and not some other, he said as he sent them forth into the future. Whenever you gather like this around the table, tell the stories of your lives and be renewed in the process. Let yourselves love with abandon and know you will heal from the hurts. You will be my Body, broken and re-membered. Heal the broken-hearted. Bring sight to the blind. Release the captives and celebrate life with this food for your souls. Be who you are meant to be. Honor me by stepping out into the future with confidence that you are created to be creators, in the likeness of God.

Epilogue

Recently I visited Jean Mideke, the wife of my mentor and friend Louie, who died in 1989. She asked me to help her look for his glaze notebooks, so she unlocked his studio, and I began looking into familiar cupboards and shelves. In his last year Louie had carefully cleaned up his tools and laid them out on the counter. Glaze jars had been emptied and washed. Samples had been sorted and labeled — the lifetime habits of a creative soul completing his journey homeward.

When I opened his storage cupboard, there were many small vases and bowls, but my eye was drawn to a beautiful brown pitcher made early in his career as a potter. I recognized it because I own one like it, which I bought in 1963. But this one was taller and slimmer than the one I had. With a narrow base and a high shoulder, it stood graceful and sure in the shadows, toward the back of the crowded shelf.

Though we did not find his notebooks, I offered to take the pitcher into the house where Jean keeps Louie's best pots. She said "No, it belongs here." But the pitcher keeps coming to the eye of my mind, and the words, "This is my body . . ." have been singing in my sleep ever since. I know that I have been given an inner guide to follow for the next part of my journey of being who I am created to be.

Is Louie's pitcher calling me back to the potter's wheel? Or is its message something about being both a container and a pouring vessel? All I know for now is that the brown pitcher, made of clay he dug from the ground and glazed with a simple brown slip, is an image to guide my soul forward, toward its source.

Index to the Biblical Monologues

MARJORY ZOET BANKSON

As President of Faith at Work, a national ministry for lay and clergy renewal, Marjory Bankson has had broad experience in developing structures and practices for deepening spiritual growth. A graduate of Radcliffe College, she also has a master's degree in history from the University of Alaska. At Dartmouth College, she served as the first women's counselor before becoming a professional potter in the 1970s. With her husband, Peter, Marjory lives in Alexandria, Virginia. She is affiliated with the Seekers, one of the worshipping communities of The Church of the Saviour in Washington, D.C. Much in demand as a conference speaker and retreat leader, she is the author of two previous books, *Braided Streams: Esther and a Woman's Way of Growing* and *Seasons of Friendship: Naomi and Ruth as a Pattern*, also published by LuraMedia.

Other LuraMedia Publications

BANKSON, MARJORY ZOET

Braided Streams:
Esther and a Woman's Way of Growing

Seasons of Friendship:
Naomi and Ruth as a Pattern

"This Is My Body. . .":
Creativity, Clay, and Change

BOHLER, CAROLYN STAHL

Prayer on Wings: *A Search for Authentic Prayer*

**DOHERTY, DOROTHY ALBRACHT
and McNAMARA, MARY COLGAN**

Out of the Skin Into the Soul:
The Art of Aging

GEIGER, LURA JANE

and **PATRICIA BACKMAN**

Braided Streams Leader's Guide

and **SUSAN TOBIAS**

Seasons of Friendship Leader's Guide

JEVNE, RONNA FAY

It All Begins With Hope:
Patients, Caretakers, and the Bereaved Speak Out

and **ALEXANDER LEVITAN**

No Time for Nonsense:
Getting Well Against the Odds

KEIFFER, ANN

Gift of the Dark Angel: *A Woman's Journey
through Depression toward Wholeness*

LODER, TED

Eavesdropping on the Echoes:
Voices from the Old Testament

Guerrillas of Grace:
Prayers for the Battle

Tracks in the Straw:
Tales Spun from the Manger

Wrestling the Light:
Ache and Awe in the Human-Divine Struggle

MEYER, RICHARD C.

One Anothering:
Biblical Building Blocks for Small Groups

MILLETT, CRAIG

In God's Image:
Archetypes of Women in Scripture

O'CONNOR, ELIZABETH

Search for Silence *(Revised Edition)*

PRICE, H.H.

Blackberry Season:
A Time to Mourn, A Time to Heal

RAFFA, JEAN BENEDICT

The Bridge to Wholeness:
A Feminine Alternative to the Hero Myth

SAURO, JOAN

Whole Earth Meditation:
Ecology for the Spirit

SCHAPER, DONNA

Stripping Down:
The Art of Spiritual Restoration

WEEMS, RENITA J.

Just a Sister Away: *A Womanist Vision
of Women's Relationships in the Bible*

The Women's Series

BORTON, JOAN

Drawing from the Women's Well:
Reflections on the Life Passage of Menopause

CARTLEDGE-HAYES, MARY

To Love Delilah:
Claiming the Women of the Bible

DUERK, JUDITH

Circle of Stones:
Woman's Journey to Herself

O'HALLORAN, SUSAN *and*
DELATTRE, SUSAN

The Woman Who Lost Her Heart:
A Tale of Reawakening

RUPP, JOYCE

The Star in My Heart:
Experiencing Sophia, Inner Wisdom

SCHNEIDER-AKER, KATHERINE

God's Forgotten Daughter:
*A Modern Midrash: What If
Jesus Had Been A Woman?*

**LuraMedia, Inc. , 7060 Miramar Rd., Suite 104, San Diego, CA 92121
Call 1-800-FOR-LURA for information about bookstores or ordering.**
Books for Healing and Hope, Balance and Justice.